Runaways:
Coping
at Home
and on the Street

PATRICIA CONNORS, A.C.S.W.,
EXECUTIVE DIRECTOR OF COVENANT
HOUSE NINELINE WITH
DORIANNE PERRUCCI

Published in 1989 by The Rosen Publishing Group, Inc.
29 East 21st Street, New York, NY 10010

Copyright 1989 by Covenant House

First Edition

Library of Congress Cataloging-in-Publication Data

Connors, Patricia.
   Runaways : coping at home and on the street/Patricia
Connors with Dorianne Perrucci.—1st ed.
     p.   cm.
   Bibliography: p.
   Includes index.
   Summary: Case studies explore the reasons why teenagers
run away from home, the dangers of living on the streets,
where to find help, and coping techniques for staying home.
   ISBN 0-8239-1019-9
   1. Runaway youth—United States—Case studies—Juvenile
literature.   2. Abused children—United States—Case stud-
ies—Juvenile literature.   3. Runaway youth—Services for—
Case studies—Juvenile literature.   4. Covenant House
(New York)—Juvenile literature. [1. Runaways.]   I. Perrucci,
Dorianne R., 1949–   . II. Title.
HV1431.C66   1989
362.7′4—dc19   89-3631
                                              CIP
                                              AC

Manufactured in the U.S.A.

A B O U T   T H E   A U T H O R ◇

Pat Connors brings a rich and varied background in helping youth to her current responsibilities as Executive Director of the Nineline. The new national toll-free hotline at Covenant House began in October, 1987. Covenant House, which was founded more than twenty years ago by Father Bruce Ritter, provides crisis intervention and counseling twenty-four hours a day, seven days a week, to all homeless and runaway youth under twenty-one.

The author worked as a teacher, child-care worker, social worker, and administrator in several child-care organizations for over twenty-five years before joining Covenant House in 1978. Ms. Connors has worked directly with the children and teenagers of Covenant House, and she has been instrumental as well in guiding the expansion of the Covenant House program into several other locations throughout the United States, Canada, and Central America.

In addition to her efforts at focusing media and public attention on the task of reaching potential runaways, Nineline's Executive Director organizes ongoing efforts in education and training to better equip the Nineline team of counselors who work with young people in crisis.

Pat Connors has a Master's Degree in Social Work

from Fordham University in New York and is a member of the Academy of Certified Social Workers. She is also a licensed social worker in the state of New York. Her real education, she says, starts with the challenge of helping America's youth and families learn how to better communicate with each other.

Acknowledgments

I would like to thank a number of my staff at Nineline who gave their time and experience by contributing information and insight that is critical to understanding and helping the young runaway. My special thanks to Ilene Gotkin, Chris Hamlin, Margaret Linton, Wendy Naidich, and Barbara Reichenthal for making this book, in the spirit of Nineline, truly a team effort.

My special thanks also to John Kells, whose vision and energy in reaching kids with effective communication *before* they run was instrumental in initiating and guiding this project to completion; and to Dorianne Perrucci, for taking my many notes, thoughts, and experiences and so ably turning them into a readable, compelling manuscript.

But most of all, I want to thank Father Bruce Ritter. For more than twenty years he has been the driving force behind our work. Because of him, thousands of kids who had no one else to turn to and no other place to go were reached in time. Thanks to his commitment, vision, and energy, Covenant House, the Nineline, and our many other programs will continue to be there in the years to come to help put kids and their families back together again.

Contents

Acknowledgments — vii

Introduction: Reaching Out for Help — 1

1 Jessica's Story—"The Running Never Stops" — 7

2 Taking a Step in the Wrong Direction — 17

3 When Family Ties Begin to Break — 24

4 Hurt by Word and Deed—Child Abuse — 34

5 Numbing the Pain—Drug and Alcohol Addiction — 46

6 An Urgent Problem—Crack — 59

7 Checking Out—Suicide — 68

8 Caving In—Peer Pressure — 77

9 How to Be Your Own Best Friend — 88

Epilogue—One Last Word — 97

Thank-yous from Kids — 99

Appendix — 105

Glossary — 115

Index — 117

Introduction: Reaching Out for Help

I was happy to take on the challenge of heading up our new national toll-free hotline in New York because I love working with kids. They are open, spontaneous, refreshing, challenging, seeking, questioning, testing, and above all, very vulnerable.

I've worked with kids for over twenty-five years in various capacities: as a teacher, a child-care worker, and even as a live-in houseparent. That's when friends of mine thought I had really lost my mind, being available for kids twenty-four hours a day! But what I realized from that experience was just how important it is for kids to know that there is someone there to help them when they need it.

Like our shelters at Covenant House, the new Nine-line operates twenty-four hours a day, seven days a week, for any youngster under twenty-one years old who needs help. If you can't stay at home because you're being abused or your life is being threatened, you may need to find a safe place to stay—but please, *don't* run to the streets! If you do, you'll run into worse problems than the one you have. The streets are absolutely the worst place you can go. They're not safe, and you can get really hurt before you realize what's happening.

Some of the kids whose stories you'll read in this book

learned that the hard way—and, sadly, some of them learned it too late. Every year thousands of kids disappear or die in this country. I don't want that to happen to you! You can get help now, *before* things get out of control. Many of the kids in this book learned how to do that, and you can, too.

First of all, you don't have to handle your problems alone. Lots of people are ready and willing to help a kid in trouble. Find someone you trust and talk to him or her. If you don't have someone you can turn to, like a neighbor or relative or teacher, ask for help from Nineline or one of the other national hotlines listed in the Appendix.

Second, it's a lot easier to get help than you think. Because we know how important it is to talk to someone when you have a problem, Nineline has twenty phone lines available. You won't have to wait very long to talk to someone about what's bothering you. Our counselors are expert at listening; Covenant House has been helping kids for more than twenty years. A Nineline counselor will stay on the line with you as long as you need to talk.

But our help doesn't stop there. We can connect you with people in your own hometown who can give you the additional help and support you might need. Each counselor's phone is hooked up to a computer that lists thousands of names and addresses and phone numbers of people and organizations all over this country who are ready and willing to help kids in trouble. Thanks to our phone system, you can have a three-way conversation with one of these people while our counselor stays on the line with you.

Third, getting help doesn't cost you anything. The

call is free, and it is also confidential, which means that you don't have to give us your name or address. Our main concern is to know that you're not in danger.

You'll be surprised to find out that you're not the first kid in the world who has run into serious problems at home and thought about running away. In our first year of operation Nineline received over one million calls from every state in the country, including Alaska and Hawaii and Puerto Rico. Most of these calls came from kids who were thinking about running away from home, but some of them, surprisingly, came from parents who were confused and upset and wanted to communicate better with their kids.

Sometimes parents don't know how to react or what to say to you. Sometimes they are too busy or bothered by something to really listen to you. And sometimes it takes an extra effort to keep the channels of communication open.

You're lucky if you have parents who are always there when needed and who try, at least most of the time, to:

- respond to you consistently;
- set fair and reasonable limits;
- keep a sense of humor;
- practice what they preach;
- and express their love, both emotionally and physically.

In all fairness to parents, nobody can hit a perfect ten all the time; it's just not possible. A certain amount of stress and strain in growing up is normal, and a certain amount of stress and strain with your parents is also normal. That's different, though, from a situation where

4 ◇ R U N A W A Y S

things get out of control. It's not normal, for instance, to be beaten until you're black and blue every time you disagree with your parents. Being disciplined is one thing; being abused is another.

Perhaps something like that is happening to you right now. You don't feel good about it, you're not sure it's normal—but you feel caught in the situation and unable to change it.

Things may be so bad, in fact, that you're beginning to think there's only one way to change them. Running away is a solution, but it's only a *temporary* one. Being out on the street is a choice, but it is absolutely the worst choice you can make. That's what thousands of kids have told us after they ended up there and came to Covenant House for help. They're sorry they made that choice— they wish they had known what would happen—things could have been a lot different if they had just stopped and thought it through—but it was too late by the time they realized that. They wished they had learned to communicate better with their parents.

That's why I'm especially glad when we get calls from parents and have the opportunity to act as a bridge between them and their kids in helping to put things back together again. Many of these families were able to work things out, and we know you can, too.

When you talk to our counselors, they'll help you in the same way we've helped thousands of kids over the years by following the "Covenant" principles. You can learn to straighten out what's wrong by looking at the decisions you're making. Good principles help you make good decisions, whereas bad principles get you into more trouble. As you talk to our counselors, you'll begin to understand what you might need to do to make a positive change in your life.

"Covenant" principles

Immediacy—You (or your family—Nineline is for both parents and kids) can call us twenty-four hours a day, seven days a week, and receive a caring and accepting response without delay.

Sanctuary—We care about you regardless of what you have done or where you have been. You don't have to tell us your name or where you are if that doesn't put you or someone else in danger.

Value Communication—"Absolute respect" and "unconditional love" are not just words at Covenant House; they are keys to positive change. You may have learned that honesty is not the best policy in order to survive out on the street or at home, but you don't have to lie to us to feel safe. We'll listen to your thoughts and feelings and not judge you. We'll also help you figure out how to talk to your family. Sometimes that means coming to grips with the fact that your family is not all you hoped for and expected. Honest and open communication is the start.

Structure—Finding a solution that fits each individual situation is our goal in answering each call that comes into Nineline. There's no "one way" we help all kids; we work with all our callers one on one to find the individual solution they need. We go step by step, listening to each of your questions and concerns. As you calm down, you can begin to figure out what you need to do.

Choice—Sometimes when you're in the middle of a

crisis it seems as if there's nothing you can do. You feel powerless and unable to control what's happening. Our counselors can help you realize that you can make good choices that will lead to the positive changes you want.

But you've got to take the first step. That's the only way things are going to change for the better.

In this book you'll read about a lot of kids who learned how to do just that. We've changed their names to protect their privacy, but we did not change their stories. Some of them had to go through some awfully painful experiences before that happened. Please listen and learn from what they have to say.

And if—just if—you don't need help, then count yourself lucky and think about passing along this book—and our phone number—to someone who really does need it. Let them know that they don't have to be alone in reaching out for help.

Pat Connors

CHAPTER 1

Jessica's Story—"The Running Never Stops"

"I never would have thought when I was growing up—I would never have thought in a million years—that this was the way I was going to be before I even turned eighteen...

"If I could just—if just one kid would stay home and try to work out the problems—if one family could just work their problems out—it would make my whole miserable life worthwhile..."

"Hello, Covenant House Nineline, can I help you?"

It was late when I got Jessica's call. At first she didn't talk, so I waited a moment. I knew from experience that someone on the other end of the phone was trying to get up the courage to start talking.

"Yeah," a young voice finally blurted, "I'm calling from a trick's house who gave me the number, isn't that weird?" (A "trick" is usually a sexual favor performed for money. Sometimes it also refers to a "john," a customer who pays for sex.) She must be in pretty bad shape, I knew, if a trick had told her to call; that doesn't happen too often.

Her name was Jessica, the girl said. That was probably her "street" name, but it didn't matter. What mattered was that she wanted to talk. She laughed, a short, bitter laugh that ended with a sob. "Oh God," she said, choking on her tears as she struggled to talk, "I'm so desperate. I don't know what to do."

She was only seventeen years old, she told me, but she had been selling herself to survive since she ran away from home three years ago. I shook my head when I heard that, not just because her story was so sad—but because it was so true. More than one million teenagers run away every year.[1] Most of them do end up going back home, but thousands of them stay on the street and are forced to turn to prostitution to survive.[2]

That's what had happened to Jessica. A lot had happened to her in the past three years that wasn't very nice at all. In fact, she told me, it was a lot worse than anything she could ever have imagined.

"I'm sorry," she kept apologizing between sobs, "I haven't talked to anyone about this since I ran away. I'm sorry to be taking up so much of your time."

"It's really okay," I said. "That's what we're here for."

Jessica cried for several more minutes before she calmed down. "I've changed so much," she said, her voice shaking. "Sometimes I don't even recognize myself. I was really pretty once." Now she had ugly track marks on her arms from the heroin she injected daily and even gray hair. "Can you imagine?" she asked.

I couldn't say anything for a moment. After all these years of working with kids, it still bothers me to realize how much some kids have to suffer.

"It must be really hard for you," I said.

"Yes," Jessica replied, starting to cry again. "Sometimes I think about killing myself. You just can't help it, you hurt so much. But you can't afford to let anyone know how you're feeling. They might rip you off or mess you up really bad. So you don't trust anyone—you can't."

"You're trusting me," I said gently; "that took a lot of courage. What made you change your mind?"

"I was really scared," Jessica said. "When I woke up in that sleazy hotel room tonight, I was so out of it, I didn't know who I was or where I was. I really scared the john I was with—he was the one who made me call you—and I scared myself. I know I have to do something, but I don't know what," she said. "And I don't know if I can. I think it's too late for me to change."

"That's how a lot of kids feel," I said. "I'm not saying it will be easy—it won't. But things can change, if you're willing to try. And I think you really want them to—you called us tonight, which took a lot of courage. That's a start."

There was a long pause on the other end of the phone. "It seems like forever since I ran away from home," Jessica said, so softly I almost didn't hear. "Three years...."

"But you probably feel as if you haven't stopped running," I said. "The running hasn't really stopped, has it? It's become a way of life."

"I never realized before," she said, "how much you run. You run from everybody and everything. You run from the drugs, from the pimps, and from the police. You run from everybody, and you just keep running and running until you finally run out." She sounded so tired as she talked.

Several years ago, Jessica's mother had remarried. At first the girl loved all the attention from her stepfather. "It was great, the way he would pull me onto his lap and wrap me in a big bear hug," she said. "After practically having grown up without a father, I really liked all the attention. But one night, when my mother was out..." Jessica was quiet for a moment before she continued. "My stepfather raped me!" she said. "I felt really confused and upset, like something bad had happened, but he kept telling me it was okay. But I didn't feel okay. He said he loved me and that people wouldn't understand, so I had to be sure not to tell anyone. That made me feel worse, like I really had done something wrong."

"He started yelling because I wouldn't stop crying. I ran to my room and locked the door, I was so scared. I could hear him screaming and swearing. I kept hoping my mother would get home soon.

"She finally came," Jessica recalled, "and I tried to tell her what had happened. She didn't say anything for a minute—and then she started laughing! She said, 'Of course, I knew he wasn't such a nice guy when I married him, but at my age I didn't have too many choices. You'll just have to learn to put up with it, as long as he stays away from me.'"

"I couldn't believe it," Jessica said, "I just couldn't believe it. It was like a nightmare. My own mother wouldn't protect me! I wasn't safe in my own house. I told myself I had to leave. I didn't have any other choice..."

The next day Jessica got up and got ready for school, but she never showed up at class. She went to the bus station instead and bought a one-way ticket for New York.

She didn't stop to think about what she was doing. She was too upset. How could she know that she wouldn't be able to find to job that would pay her enough to live? Or that no one would rent an apartment to her because she was too young? The only thing she was thinking about, the only thing she knew, was that she had to get away. Everything would be okay once she got away from home, she told herself. Things would change.

They did, almost from the moment she stepped off the bus—but not in the way she had imagined.

Everything was so confusing that she didn't know what to do. She had never seen so many people before, and it seemed that all of them were rushing around and bumping into her to get someplace in a hurry. It was scary, being somewhere where nobody knew your name.

Jessica tried to look as though she knew what she was doing, like she had a place to go, too, so she stopped and bought a soda and a slice of pizza. She was standing there wondering where she could stay for the night and how much she would have to pay when someone spoke to her.

"Hey," the girl standing next to her said again, "Hi, how are you?" Jessica looked at the girl carefully. She was pretty and dressed in a nice pair of jeans and a sweater. "My name is Michelle," said the girl, who looked to be about her age, "you new here?" Before she knew it, Jessica was talking to the stranger as if she were a friend from back home.

"I know just how you feel," Michelle said sympathetically as the young runaway poured out her story. "Hey, listen, I've got this great place where I live with a bunch of other girls—why don't you come stay with us? Really, you've got to, we have so much room." Jessica was so relieved. She didn't really know Michelle, but she was so nice, and if it was okay with the rest of the girls. . . .

That was her introduction to the world of prostitution. Michelle—that "nice girl" Jessica had met at the bus station—was really a prostitute, and the apartment she took Jessica to—the one she said belonged to her uncle— really belonged to her pimp. The girl knew from experience that kids like Jessica were perfect targets for being picked up: Alone and afraid on the street, they're desperate for a place to stay and someone to pay attention to them. That's what hooked Jessica.

At first her new friend's "uncle" gave her a lot of attention. To Jessica, he acted like a real uncle—only better. He had a nice apartment and lots of money, and they went out to eat in restaurants. Most of all, he treated her kindly, and that was really important to Jessica after what she had been through. How glamorous and exciting it all was! She was feeling really happy and safe until "Uncle" let her know one day that it was time to pay him back for all the money he had spent on her. He slapped her hard when she tried to leave and locked her in the room. What could she do? She had to stay and do what he said. She had no other place to go—and she couldn't go back home. She thought she had no other choice.

So Jessica went to work in Manhattan's high-class hotels, where she attracted lots of attention because she was so young and so pretty. She bought fancy clothes on Fifth Avenue, had lots of friends, and took taxis to work. She was making lots of money for her pimp because she was a "hot" property, and in return he gave her lots of attention. He even escorted Jessica to her "appointments" in the hotels where she worked.

The young runaway had made one big mistake by leaving home without a safe place to go, and now she made another. To keep her up all night—and to keep her making money for him—her pimp started feeding her drugs: speed to keep her awake; downers to help her sleep after all the speed; cocaine to get her up and build her confidence; and heroin to ease her down again. She was really getting hooked, but by then she was too sucked into "the life" to notice—and that's when the slide downward accelerated.

After a while, she went from working the big hotels to smaller and seedier ones, and finally she ended up on the street, where the prostitutes work for $5 and $10 a trick instead of the hundreds Jessica was used to making. She began to feel more and more worthless when nobody wanted to pay top dollar for her anymore. That's how much the street had twisted her values.

"I think it's too late for me," she said, starting to cry again.

"That's what a lot of kids think," I said, "but it's never too late to get your life together. If you had called us three years ago, we would have found a safe place where you could stay, a temporary shelter or even a foster home. And there are choices you can make right now."

"Really?" she asked. "Like what? I mean, how do you think you would be able to help me? Do you really think you could, after what I've done?"

"Why don't you talk to a counselor over at Covenant House yourself?" I asked. "You can ask any questions you like, and I'll still be on the line with you," I explained; "our phone system lets us have three-way conversations."

In a moment I heard Ernie pick up the phone. "Ernie," I said, "this is Jessica. Jessica, Ernie." Everyone laughed over the unusual "introductions."

"Hi, Ernie," Jessica said. "Hi, Jessica, how are you?" Ernie asked. "Well..." the girl began, taking a big breath. She had a lot of questions, she told Ernie. "That's okay," he said, "go ahead."

"Will the other kids laugh at me when they know what I've been doing?" Jessica wanted to know. "They won't know," Ernie said. "They don't have to unless you want to tell them." "That's a relief," Jessica said.

"What about going home?" she asked next. "Do I have to?"

"That doesn't sound like such a good idea," Ernie said, "unless your mother and stepfather are willing to get some help for their problem, and we're sure you'll be safe."

"How long can I stay with you?" Jessica asked anxiously.

"Until we're able to make sure you have a safe place to live," Ernie reassured her, "whether that's eventually home or independent living. In the meantime, we'll help you go back to school or help you figure out what to do first. We'll help you in any way we can."

Jessica sounded more relaxed. "Where do I sleep?" she wanted to know.

"With other girls your age. The rooms are on a floor, like in a dorm," Ernie described, "do you know what I mean?"

"Not really," Jessica said, "you mean like a big hotel?"

"In a way," Ernie said, "only they're a lot nicer. Our places are a lot like a home, you know."

"Oh," Jessica said quietly. Then she asked, "Do I have to be in at a certain time?"

"I'm afraid so," Ernie said, laughing, "we have a pretty stiff curfew, but it's only because we want you to be safe, and the streets around here can be pretty dangerous."

"That will probably take some getting used to," Jessica said. "I mean, having someone watch out for me. But I think I could get used to feeling safe."

Then she paused and took a big breath. "I'm feeling better now," she told me, "but I'm really tired."

"We would love for you to come and stay with us," I said. "You could come tonight. We could arrange for some of our staff to pick you up. We have a special van that goes out on the street to help kids."

"I know," she said, "I've seen it. But I just need some time to think things through. You've given me a lot to think about. But it's a big step for me, getting off the street."

"I know," I said. "It will take a lot of hard work—but I think you can do it. Maybe now you understand that you can change things for yourself—and that's the most important thing. You took a big step tonight, having the courage to ask for help."

"Thanks," she said, "but you made it easy by listening to me. Don't worry, I won't forget your number, 1-800-999-9999." She paused again. "I just wish I had known about Covenant House before I ran away."

"We wish all kids did," I said, "because nobody can believe how awful it can be out on the street."

CHAPTER ◊ 2

Taking a Step in the Wrong Direction

"*I love my father,*" *said fifteen-year-old Tina from Los Angeles, "but I don't think I can take it anymore! I feel sorry that he's stuck in a wheelchair since his accident, but he drinks all day long and I have to skip school to take care of him since my mother left.*"

Fourteen-year-old Joanne was calling from a small town in Texas. She had just come home to pick up her bike, she told our Nineline counselor, and then she was leaving forever. Her mother had punched her yesterday after the girl had tried to inject herself with insulin. "I understand that my little brother is a diabetic and needs extra attention, but I'm sick and tired of him getting all of it," she said.

Hundreds of miles away, up north in Chicago, nineteen-year-old Robert was feeling just as lonely as Joanne, but there was one big difference: He had never known his parents. From the time he was a baby Robert had been passed from one relative to the next until he got tired of belonging to no one and ran to the streets looking for someone to love him. He did, but it was the wrong kind of love...

What do you think about runaways and homeless kids? That they're troublemakers? Kids who really don't have serious problems? Kids who can go back home if things don't work out?

Is it possible that kids run away because they just don't know what else to do?

Could you or someone you know, in fact, be thinking about running away because that's the only way you can deal with problems you're having at home?

Who runs away?

According to a report published in 1987 by the Runaway and Homeless Youth Program, a federal program that provides temporary shelters for runaways, all kinds of kids run away; there is no one "type." Kids who run away come from all kinds of backgrounds.[3] So the odds are pretty high that sometime during your teen years you or someone you know will take that step, because one in every twelve kids runs away before the age of eighteen.[4]

In most states, a *runaway* is a young person under eighteen years old who leaves home or a place of residence without the permission of parents or legal guardians. Although most of the kids stranded on the street are runaways (88 percent), some kids are *homeless* (11 percent). More specifically, these homeless kids are "throwaways" or "pushouts," which means they don't have a place to go home to because their parents or guardians no longer want them.

Runaways can be younger, but the average age is fifteen or sixteen (47 percent). Most of them are girls (57 percent). The majority are white (69 percent). Black kids (17 percent), Hispanic kids (8 percent), and Native American or Asian kids (6 percent) run away, too, but in far fewer numbers.

The good news is that more than half of these young runaways travel less than ten miles from home, and they don't stay away too long: Most are gone less than a few days before returning to relatives or friends (68 percent). Others are placed in foster homes or in some other type of stable living situation (26 percent).

The bad news outweighs the good. The longer a youngster stays on the street, the harder it is to return home. Only 6 percent of all kids who run away return to the street. But if you figure out the math, that means as many as 60,000 kids every year are stranded on the street with no place to go.

Worse than that, the statistics show that a lot of kids *keep on* running away from home: 14 percent had run away once before; 22 percent had run away two to four times before; and 16 percent had run away more than five times![5] In other words, kids keep running away because they haven't found a way to solve their problems at home.

For a kid who is stranded on the street and doesn't get help fast, the odds of getting hurt are very high. The danger you face is like a time bomb waiting to go off. Maybe even worse, the warped values you learn on the street will make it that much harder for you to straighten out your life.

So take a closer look. You may begin to realize that you or someone you know has a problem at home that needs immediate attention.

Why do kids run away?

Kids leave home because they feel they have to. That's what they tell us when they call the Covenant House Nineline. The problems they face at home seem over-whelming and inescapable. They feel they have no choice but to run away.

Since Nineline began, we've talked to thousands of kids who have told us the reasons that push them out the door and into the street. We'll discuss the details in greater depth in the following chapters, but right now here's a brief description of some of the warning signs you should look for. If they are happening to you or some-one you know, pay attention to them and think about getting help before the situation gets out of control.

Family problems. Every family experiences different pressures; parents separate or divorce, a stepparent moves in, a new baby arrives, someone dies, financial worries escalate, you move to a new place, someone in your family becomes addicted to drugs or alcohol. All of these changes can strain the ties between family members. Some families learn to deal effectively with these strains; some do not. There's no magic formula for working out relationships with the people in your family. Left unresolved, family stresses and strains can build up to the point where they will finally explode and make you do something very serious—like running away to escape from the problems.

Child abuse. Child abuse is probably the most common reason why kids think about leaving home. Child abuse happens when a parent or stepparent or relative hurts a child under seventeen years old, either physically, sexually, or emotionally. Physical or sexual abuse can be a one-time occurrence, whereas emotional abuse happens repeatedly over a period of time.

Drug and alcohol abuse. Sometimes you can "run away" without even leaving home. Some people think drinking and drugs will help you deal with what's bothering you, but they don't help—in fact, they can make the problem worse. Drugs may take away the pain for a while, but you may end up addicted to drugs or alcohol. Some kids complain that it's hard to "just say no," and they're right. It is hard. Just saying no to drugs and drinking is hard if that's all you do: You need to follow up your words with action and a change in the way you act. Getting support and counseling will be critical in helping you make that change.

Suicide. Everybody feels down at times; that's normal. It's even normal for you to go up and down with some regularity; it's part of the process of growing up. Some teenagers find it harder and harder to "snap out of it," and they dwell on thoughts that are not healthy. You can even begin to think of "getting out" by either running away or committing suicide. Just remember that suicide is a permanent solution to a temporary problem, and running away can actually run you into worse problems. Both are dead-end choices.

Peer pressure. We all want to be popular and well liked, but sometimes it's not easy to go along with your friends, especially when it comes to sex. You have to learn to think for yourself and make the decisions that will be good for you. Caving in to pressure in this area may be one of the worst mistakes you can ever make. Getting AIDS or becoming pregnant as a result of depending on your friends can hurt you for the rest of your life.

Give yourself a break and take the time you need to think about these questions and answer them for yourself.

"So what should I do? I feel so desperate . . ."

The street is absolutely the worst place to work out your problems. You may be able to take care of yourself, but you're not ready to be out on the street on your own. The price you will pay to learn that lesson is very high. And you will end up paying with your life.

You won't recognize yourself after a while. You'll be a different person—and probably not someone you like at all—because the only way you can survive on the streets is to learn to use others before they use you. But you'll be too busy to notice that change.

You'll be spending so much of your time worrying about how to make it day to day that you won't realize the risks you're taking. But chances are, you'll make one of the following mistakes sooner or later:

- Sell yourself to a "sick trick" (a customer who buys you for sex and then kills or maims you).
- End up in jail. That happens to a lot of kids after they run out of money and start stealing to survive.
- Die from overdosing on drugs or alcohol. (One

bad habit feeds another: Selling yourself to survive is so awful that most kids who end up on the
street start drinking or taking drugs to forget.)

Kids who sell themselves on the street always face the
risk of getting sick, especially from sexually transmitted
diseases (STD) such as gonorrhea or syphilis. These
street diseases can be uncomfortable, but they can be
cured. Lately, though, a lot of the street kids who come
to us are testing positive for the AIDS virus—and we
can't help them. The truth is, kids who live on the street
face one of the highest risks for getting AIDS.[6] By the
time they realize that, it's too late to help them: The
AIDS virus is in their system, and sooner or later they
will die.

"Oh, come on," you say. "You're just trying to scare
me. Aren't you exaggerating?"

If anything, the reality is much worse. The stories you
will read in the next chapter are based not on what I
know, but on what the kids who have lived them know
firsthand. They learned it the hard way, by living—and
sometimes dying—on the street.

Despite the different backgrounds they come from,
these young runaways will tell you the same thing when
it comes to living on the street: The street is no place to
work out your problems. The best time to get help for
something that is bothering you at home is now, *before*
you run away, *before* things get out of control.

CONCLUSION

CHAPTER 3

When Family Ties
Begin to Break

A lot of people wonder why "Family Ties" and "The Bill Cosby Show" are so popular. True, these TV shows have a lot of laughter and some great characters. The scenes between Mr. and Mrs. Keaton, former "flower children" from the 1960s, and their eldest son, Alex, an aspiring yuppie of the '80s, can be very funny.

What makes "Family Ties" so popular, though, is the way the characters make a serious point while being funny. You have to learn to communicate: That's the basic message of the show. The Keatons struggle with the same feelings of confusion and hurt and anger that the rest of us do, but they do it a lot better than most of us. That's why we keep tuning in week after week.

We're all hoping we could be a little more like the Keatons and Cosbys. A lot of families I know actually are, but they work hard to achieve that; they've learned there's no such thing as "instant" communication. They know it takes a lot of hard work to keep a family together.

Unfortunately, some kids don't have families like that; their families are literally falling apart because they haven't learned to listen to each other. The kids in these families are ready to run because they think that leaving home is the only way they can escape what's happening there.

Running away actually looks like their only choice after a while. Of course, it's not; running away only runs you into *worse* problems.

But you don't know that when things get out of control at home. All you know is that you want help *now*. Well, you can get it—if you're willing to learn how to stay and cope with your problem instead. That's the basic message "Family Ties" dramatizes every week.

It's a lot better to stay and face what's bothering you than to run away from it and to the street. You *can* get the help you need by learning how to take a step in the right direction instead.

Let's see how a girl from California who called me recently learned to do just that.

"What can I do?"

"Hello, Covenant House Nineline," I said, "can I help you?"

The girl started crying when she heard that.

"I. . ."

"Yes," I said, "go ahead. By the way, my name is Pat."
I could hear noise in the background, like a washing machine running. I wasn't surprised: Kids call Nineline from all sorts of locations. Our caller had sought the

privacy of the family laundry room so that no one could hear her. Her voice was very soft and quiet as she began again, but it started shaking as she tried to get the words out. "My name is Tina," she began. "I don't know what to do. I just can't stand it anymore," she blurted out, "I'm thinking about running away." And then she hung up.

I hoped she would call back. It takes a lot of courage for some of the kids who call us to pick up the phone, and sometimes a few tries before they stay on the line with us.

The next day at about the same time, the phone rang again. One of the other Nineline counselors motioned me over. "Someone is asking for you," she said.

"Hi, it's Tina, remember me?"

"Yes, yes I do. How are you today?"

"A little better, but not much," the teenager said honestly. "Yesterday I had had a big fight with my father when I called you. I was too upset to talk. It's still bad today, but now I think I can talk. Besides, he's sleeping."

"He's sleeping because he's drunk again," the fifteen-year-old continued. "I love him, but I don't think I can take it anymore! I don't know what to do. I feel sorry that he's stuck in a wheelchair since his accident, but he drinks all day long and I have to skip school a lot to take care of him since my mother left. . . ." She started crying and couldn't stop for a while.

"It's okay," I kept reassuring her, "I'm still here."

She told the rest of her story between sobs as she slowly calmed down. Nine years ago Tina's father was in a terrible car accident that left him disabled. Unable to work, confined to a wheelchair, he began drinking a few years ago as a way of dealing with his frustration. The problem was that he couldn't or wouldn't stop. He didn't seem to want to.

At first Tina thought she could help him. "Actually, I didn't seem to have much of a choice," she said defensively. "My mother left two years ago; she couldn't take it." Tina tried to understand why her father started drinking. "He was so frustrated," she said. "Who wouldn't be? Being stuck in a wheelchair for the rest of your life?"

Despite all her efforts, her father wasn't getting any better; in fact, things were just getting worse, and she was having a hard time understanding why. "I tried so hard," Tina said, starting to cry again. "Wasn't I good enough?" Instead of thanking her or being the slightest bit cooperative, her father lashed out at her with unkind words and accusations that hurt more than seeing him drunk most of the time. "You're lazy," he'd tell Tina. "And you're stupid. Can't you do anything right?"

"Sometimes he's his old self," she said. "We even play cards and joke, but mostly it's like he's gone. I feel like he died in that car wreck. I don't know what to do anymore."

Tina was right: Sometimes her father was there, sometimes he wasn't. A parent who drinks or abuses drugs is a real Dr. Jekyll and Mr. Hyde; he constantly changes as a result of the addiction, shifting from normal to abnormal behavior in a matter of minutes.

Tina was skipping school and getting sick as a result of her father's problem, but that wasn't the worst part. She was feeling more and more worthless and insecure because she was failing to help him. The more she tried, in fact, the worse he seemed to get—and the worse she felt. She worried about him so much that the pressure

was taking a toll on her health. She wasn't eating very
well, and most nights she hardly slept. "I don't know if
I'm too young," she said, "but I'm wondering: Can a kid
have a nervous breakdown? Because I think I might be
having one."

"That isn't hard to understand at all," I told her.
"Trying to take responsibility for someone else's problem
can really hurt you in the end. The constant fighting
and arguments that go on put tremendous strain and
discontent on everyone in the family—especially you."
Even if you're not the target of the abuse as Tina was,
you can still suffer just by being part of the situation.
And after a while you may start looking for a way out
too.

"Well, that's where things are at," Tina said. "I don't
know what to do. I really don't want to run away. Crazy
as it sounds, I love my father. I know leaving home
would help me forget everything that's happening, but
then I know I would miss him. Where would I go? How
would I get there? And what would happen to me? I'd
have to live on the street," the girl said, "and I don't
think I'd like that at all. I've heard about what happens
to a kid with no place to go. I think I'd be scared to be
out on the street. I don't know how I would make it."
She hesitated a moment. "No, thanks," she concluded.

"But how can I keep going?" Tina asked. "This situation is making me sick."

"You don't have to live with the situation as it is," I
answered, "you've already realized that. Running yourself down is really bad. It will make you feel even worse
about yourself."

"How much worse can that be?" Tina asked.

"Believe me, it can get a lot worse," I said. "The

relationship with your father could deteriorate to the point where one of you does something you'd really regret. I'm glad you stopped and thought about it first. You've taken a step to help yourself by calling us."

"I do feel a lot better," Tina admitted, "but my situation hasn't changed."

"Okay," I said. "What you need now is someone close by who can help you straighten out your situation or learn to deal with it better. Is there anybody you can talk to—an aunt or a cousin, maybe?"

"Not really," Tina said.

"Well, there are people who could help you figure out what to do. The kind of people I'm talking about," I explained, "are people who can handle it. People who are experienced at helping families who are having problems."

"Like who?" Tina said, a little defensively. "I'm not sure I want anyone to see how bad my father is."

"What I can do right now is see what agencies and programs are available in your area to give you some counseling and support. I think in your situation the local family services agency could send in a homemaker so you could feel okay about leaving your father and going to school. There may be some organization that works with handicapped people that he could join for social and recreational activities. And counseling for both of you would probably be good too, especially for your father's drinking problem. You could also go to Alateen, which is for teenagers like you who are trying to figure out what to do about a parent's problem."

"Oh," Tina said. "I didn't realize all that could be possible."

"If you'll hold on, I'll make a call and see who's available in your area." In a matter of minutes Tina was talking to a counselor from an agency not too far from her home, and they had made an appointment to talk in person the next day. In the meantime, I encouraged Tina to call us back if she needed to.

"Well," said Tina, as our conversation came to a close, "thanks again. Things don't look nearly as hopeless as I thought. I think it will take a lot of work, but that's a whole lot better than letting things get worse."

Taking the next step

Tina's father's disability led to his drinking, which led him to abuse her emotionally. Left unresolved, each problem got worse and worse until it created another. A lot of the kids who call us for help are dealing with more than one problem.

Tina didn't want to leave her father, but she couldn't handle the responsibility of taking care of him on her own any longer. Should she leave home and leave her father, whom she still loved? If she stayed, how could she deal with the pressure? What about school? And her future? It's not hard to understand why getting out looked like the easiest solution to her.

What would you have told Tina? What would you tell yourself or a friend in the same situation?

Family conflicts are the most common reason why kids who call Nineline leave or think about leaving home. A certain amount of stress and strain is a normal part of growing up. If you're facing a problem at home, though, don't wait until it explodes into a crisis and pushes you out the door.

The kids whose stories you'll read in this book learned

how to stay and cope with their problem—and you can too. You can start by recognizing the "warning signs" that tell you it's time to get help.

Recognizing the signs

A parent who has a drug or alcohol problem. A parent who drinks to excess hurts himself or herself and everyone else in the family. At the least, such parents can act silly or embarrass their family in public. At the worst, they may abuse a spouse or child physically or emotionally when they're drunk.

It doesn't matter what kind of abuse happens; the result is still the same: This parent has a problem that is causing everyone to suffer.

A parent, stepparent, brother, or sister who abuses a child. Youngsters who are being abused can feel very confused and guilty: They want to stop hurting, but they're afraid the adult who is hurting them will be hurt too. They want to tell someone what is happening, but they're afraid that the person abusing them may go to jail as a result or even try to "get back" at them.

They may also feel that it is their fault the abuse is happening.

And they may be ashamed to admit that they still love the person who is abusing them. This is not unusual, because the abuser is likely to be their own mother, father, stepparent, sibling, or some other relative or adult they have known their entire life.

There are many reasons why people abuse children. A lot of the time, they have been victims of child abuse themselves, and they can only treat someone else the way they have been treated. Regardless of the reason, it is important to remember that the abuse is **not** the victim's fault.

Fighting between parent and child. Things are out of control at home when a lot of screaming and fighting and hitting goes on. This is not the normal way that families deal with stressful situations and conflicts.

A major family change that puts pressure on a family. Parents feel tremendous anxiety when they can't provide their family with the basic necessities. Food and clothing budgets as well as tempers get stretched to the breaking point and snap when resources are limited. If a parent loses a job, things at home can get pretty tense.

A lot of anxiety is created when parents separate or divorce. The parent left behind now has to assume sole responsibility for running the household, as well as managing the upset everyone is going through. If the main breadwinner is gone, there may also be unexpected financial stress. If a parent remarries, family members can feel anxious and insecure about dealing with this new relationship.

The teens may develop their own problems as a way of dealing with the pressure. They may turn to other ways besides running away to "get away," such as drinking and doing drugs.

A parent or sibling who is ill or dying. If someone at home is seriously ill, everyone can suffer as a result. Children or teenagers may feel it's their fault. As a result, they don't talk about the sick person's condition to their friends, and they avoid bringing anyone home. In addition, youngsters may also be taking on extra responsibility to keep things together, especially if a parent is involved. Teenagers need their parents for support and guidance, but instead, it's the other way around: The parents rely on their child.

Learning to cope with your problems

You may need to get help from someone outside the family if there are problems at home. You have a right to feel angry and upset, but it's what you do with those feelings that either helps or hurts you.

Remember, you can't run away from your problems. A lot of kids think they can. If you believe that and decide to run, you will end up "getting back" at someone, all right—yourself.

Hurt by Word and Deed—Child Abuse

I n 1985, 18 percent of the kids who left home said that they had run away because they were being abused.

Just two years later that statistic had jumped to a frightening 61 percent, and the young runaways interviewed revealed that more than half of the abuse was inflicted by their own parents![7]

As upsetting as this fact is, I think it's good that more and more kids today are asking for help—and that more and more people are realizing that kids do need help, especially when it comes to abuse. You can't get away from the problem by just leaving home. The effects of being abused will stay with you for the rest of your life. The secret you try to hide will only end up twisting your values and influencing your relationships with people, especially adults.

If you have been abused, you can begin to believe that

the only way for someone to express love for you is to abuse you. After a while you'll expect every adult in the world to abuse you because of what you've suffered. Even after you grow up, years later, you can still be so hurt by what happened to you as a child that you won't let anyone get close to you. You can still feel that you'll be hurt or even killed if you let anyone get to know you. To protect yourself, you push people away, and when you feel isolated you believe you're not a worthwhile person anyway.

Most abused kids need to find some way to survive these feelings—or stop them. Some kids try to escape this vicious circle by withdrawing more and more from the difficult and painful world they find at home. They cut themselves off from having feelings of any kind, or they spend much of their time thinking about hurting themselves. To end the abuse, others think about running away.

These are false ways of coping, and they accomplish only one thing: They continue to hurt you and make you feel that you're not good enough to receive help.

That was the fear that both Jake and Alicia faced. They had learned to live with abuse from their parents since they were babies, but as they got older they decided they wanted things to be different.

That's where their stories diverge. Alicia finally went to a neighbor for help, while Jake ran to the street.

Jake's story

"I'm okay," the boy insisted, "I've got a place to stay. It ain't so bad. Besides," he added stubbornly, "it's better than home."

I could just imagine what Jake's new "home" was like—probably a space on the floor in some deserted building. "It ain't so bad," Jake said, "and I've got company, a few other kids like me. We get along fine. And we watch out for each other."

Loud laughter and a barrage of street sounds hit my ears. Sirens wailed while cars and trucks and motorcycles gunned their engines and Jake's friends laughed and partied in the background. The thirteen-year-old was calling from the notorious "Strip" in Hollywood, California. Hollywood, a mecca for would-be movie stars—and a magnet like many other places for runaway kids.

"I can't go home," Jake said. "My father wouldn't stop hitting me. I put up with it for years, because I didn't want him to beat up on my mother. But finally I couldn't stand it anymore. So I left."

He and his friends stole to keep themselves alive. "We're pretty good at it—and we haven't gotten caught yet," he added proudly.

"I'm really concerned that you'll get into a lot of trouble that way," I said.

"Nothing bad has happened to me," he said angrily.

His story was a familiar one: Most of the kids who run away do so because they are being abused. What they don't realize at the time is that they haven't left the abuse behind. They carry these old experiences with them, and after a while they meet up with new abuse on the street. The experience affects them in many ways: In Jake's case it had already twisted his values and made him afraid to trust people, especially adults.

When I told him that stealing was a risky way to try to survive, he got upset and started yelling. "I can't believe it! You want me to go back home!" he said. "You don't know what it's like! I'm not going back!"

"I'm not saying you should go home if home isn't safe," I answered, "but being on the street isn't safe either."

"You don't care—nobody does," Jake said bitterly, "and it doesn't matter anyway. I can't make my father change. There's nothing I can do."

If Jake stays out on the street too much longer, he will find it harder and harder to ignore the choices that a kid with no place to go is forced to make; stealing is just the beginning. Then comes selling drugs—or selling yourself—to survive.

Maybe the worst thing about living on the street is how fast you get old. Ever heard the expression "old before your time"? That means old in the sense of giving up on life. That's the worst—giving up your chance to be happy.

"I don't care," Jake said. "I'm doing okay." And then he hung up abruptly.

If everything was so great, I asked myself, why did Jake call in the first place? He wasn't being honest with himself. Maybe he couldn't be, right now. I hoped he would call back. Sadly, I hung up the phone.

Alicia's story

She sounded uncertain when she first asked the question.

"Is it normal for my stepfather to hit me just because I didn't do the dishes?" Alicia asked. "I know that I should have done the dishes," she admitted, "but is that any reason for him to hit me so hard that my nose bleeds? It isn't the first time," she added softly.

The twelve-year-old was calling from a neighbor's house, where she had fled after her stepfather had beaten her. Over the years she had run there often, for her stepfather said she needed a lot of "discipline."

When she was younger she thought he must be right; he was an adult, after all, and she was just a kid. But she sure needed a lot of "discipline," she recalled: regular beatings and bruisings and bloody noses.

As she got older she began talking back. "I just can't take it anymore," she said, sounding more and more upset as she talked. "I'm sick and tired of living like this. I'm sick and tired of being told I'm bad all the time. My mother says she understands, but she also says I have to put up with him—doesn't she love me?" she said, starting to cry again.

Alicia felt confused and guilty. It looked as though she had to put her mother first or herself. "I've got to think about it some more," she said between sobs. "I'll call you back tomorrow."

What is child abuse?

Child abuse, sometimes called child maltreatment, is a serious form of trouble that happens in some families. It may happen only once, but even then it is enough of a problem to get help for, especially if a serious injury or sexual incident occurs. Once child abuse starts, it often continues unless outside help is obtained.

Child abuse happens when a parent, stepparent, relative, or older sibling harms a child under seventeen physically, sexually, or emotionally, or takes advantage of the child in ways that cause injury.

There are three types of child abuse:

Physical abuse usually happens when a parent injures a child during punishment or fighting incidents. The harm caused may include visible injuries (black and blue marks, welts, bruises, cuts, burns, broken or displaced bones, and swelling); or invisible ones that must be seen in X rays (internal bleeding or torn soft tissue such as muscles). Pain, dizziness, or fainting can be signs of internal injury.

Sometimes physical abuse can include a "near miss" incident when the child was able to duck or move quickly and thus escape serious harm.

Sexual abuse happens when a parent or stepparent or adult harms you by involving you in any type of sexual activity. This includes many types of kissing (like on or in your mouth or on or in your genital area). For girls, the genitals are the vagina and internal parts that lead into the uterus. For boys, the genitals are the penis and the skin and testes, or balls, surrounding the penis.

Sexual abuse also means touching, stroking, or rubbing on or near your genitals, rectum, or breasts. It even includes situations in which a child is asked or forced to watch an adult masturbate or watch adults have intercourse. It includes being asked or forced to have sexual intercourse in any way. Sexual abuse also includes being asked or forced to touch an adult in any of the ways described.

In sexual abuse a child may not be physically injured. This is especially true if the adult does not use force. Since these parts of our bodies are clothed most of the time, no one may notice what has happened to you and you may think about ignoring what happened—but don't! Infection can still be passed along. Medical attention is particularly urgent if any bleeding, staining, burning, itching pain, or fever occurs. These are warning signals; don't ignore them. For adolescent girls, pregnancy is always a risk. If you start vomiting, feel nauseated, gain weight, or get a bloated belly, you may be pregnant.

Even when infection, bruising, or pregnancy don't occur, sexual abuse can hurt you in other ways. Such harm may show up soon after the incident, or it may not show up for years. These signs or symptoms are more emotional: feeling ashamed or embarrassed about your body; worrying constantly about your health; being too afraid or too depressed to make or keep friends; being afraid to date; or not being able to concentrate in school.

Emotional abuse occurs when a parent or stepparent uses words and feelings to strike out and embarrass, shame, or reject you. It is different from physical or sexual abuse in one very important way: It is never a one-time incident. This kind of abuse happens for months and years as the damage accumulates. Unfortunately, by the time you know that, you may already be having a lot of difficulty coping with life. This shows up in different ways: not being able to make or keep friends; not being able to pass at school; being physically sick all the time without a medical cause; or feeling very depressed.

The difference between discipline and abuse, or affection and abuse

When punishment, or discipline, becomes excessive, it becomes abuse. Excessive punishment means that you are injured. Discipline should not physically injure you.

An angry word is one thing; an endless stream of insults and put-downs by your parent is another.

You may also suffer from abuse if your parent or step-parent is too physically "affectionate" with you. It is not normal for parents and children to express feelings of love and affection for each other in romantic, sexual ways.

Why does child abuse happen?

Experts in the fields of psychology, medicine, and social work have a lot of explanations for child abuse. The most common theory is that abuse happens when stress piles up in a family in a way that becomes too much for a parent to handle. Stress can affect parents and their children in different ways.

A parent may be having stress at work, or worrying about money, or adjusting to someone new in your home such as a relative who needs to live with you or a new baby.

Children and teenagers can also suffer from stress. Even small events can stir up feelings that are upsetting or frightening to you, such as having a test at school in a subject you don't like, or not being invited to a party with your friends.

These stresses can pile up and finally explode. Maybe you miss the school bus or you get into a fight with your sister. As a result, your parents strike out at you.

Most of the time, parents don't plan or want to hurt you. Sometimes they just can't help it if they are facing a problem of their own. Many parents who abuse their children were victims of child abuse themselves, and they can only treat others the way they have been treated.

But if they begin to abuse you everytime something is bothering them, that is unfair. You don't deserve to be treated that way.

What went wrong?

Youngsters who are being abused often blame themselves for what is happening. There are at least three reasons for this.

First, parents tell children that they deserve to be abused because they did something wrong. Many, if not most, younger children believe this because they believe that whatever their parents say must be true. But that thinking is incorrect.

Second, kids blame themselves because in some way it's easier and less confusing. By blaming yourself you may think that you can change the situation. Your parent has the problem and can't change, but you can.

Third, it's less painful to believe *you're* the one who's wrong. After all, you depend on your parents for love and protection. It's pretty scary to think that the same person you need so much may be hurting you. So you hunt for a way to live in the situation, and one way is to think, "It is all my fault. I deserve this. My parents are right."

That's why abused kids try so hard to make sure no one knows, and that's why their parents may spend a lot of time making sure they can "explain" their injuries to anyone who asks ("I fell off my bike." "The dog bit me." "I walked into the door.")

After a while, though, it becomes harder and harder to hide your secret from other people—and yourself.

And that's when you have to do something to change your situation.

Sadly, a lot of kids decide to run away. It's not hard to understand why: It can seem a lot easier than facing somebody who's causing you a lot of pain.

Alicia didn't feel very comfortable calling us and "complaining," she said, but she just couldn't take it anymore. She also felt lonely and frightened, especially because "complaining" meant that she might hurt her mother. "We need him here," she had told Alicia over and over again. "Don't cause me any problems." So Alicia had learned to live with it—until this latest incident, when her stepfather had punched her and made her nose bleed. "I'm sick of going to school looking like this and lying about what happened," the girl told our counselor. Her injuries were never severe enough to put her in the hospital:—her stepfather was careful about that—just painful enough to make her feel humiliated and embarrassed and frightened.

But Alicia was sick of feeling that way. She ran next door to a neighbor who had given her shelter nearly every time her stepfather beat her. It was hard getting involved in a family's matters, but this time the woman was really alarmed: Alicia didn't want to go back home, but she couldn't stay with her either; the woman knew she wouldn't be able to protect Alicia. Sooner or later, the stepfather would come banging on the door.

What could they do? They were at a real crossroads. Something had to change. Then the neighbor remembered a commercial she had seen on TV advertising a twenty-four-hour phone counseling service from Covenant House for kids and their families who were having problems at home. She held her breath and picked up the phone.

The next step...

"Well, Alicia," the counselor told the girl when she called back, "the first thing you need to do is get to a safe place. It would be better for you not to go home tonight. Is there anyone you can stay with, a relative or friend of the family?"

"My grandmother," Alicia answered; "she knows what happens at home. I've stayed with her lots of times. She'll take me in."

"That's great," said the counselor. "Can you stay with her as long as you need?"

"I think she'll understand," the girl said calmly. "She doesn't like having to let me go back home after a while, but she always does because she doesn't know what else to do."

"Alicia, there are people whose job it is to protect children from being abused. If you're willing to make a report to such people, they may be able to make it possible for you to stay with your grandmother while they talk to you and your mother and your stepfather about what's happening. Do you think you want to talk to someone like that? It sounds to me that you feel it's important for you to stop being abused and feeling bad about yourself. We can both talk to them together if that's what you want to do—but it's going to take a lot of courage."

And it did. The social worker at the agency almost scared Alicia into changing her mind again. "Do you realize," the worker said bluntly, "what the consequences are if you're lying?" Some adults sound as if they think it's the kid's fault for being abused, but they really just need to be sure. That's because some kids exaggerate what's happening at home to get attention, or they get confused and say their parents are abusing them when they're really just disciplining them.

It is scary to stand up and say something isn't right at home, and in front of total strangers. That's why it's so important to have someone you can rely on, as Alicia did, who will be there and help you through the process of being helped.

When things seriously get out of control at home, you can't solve your problems on your own. You need some outside help. In the Appendix we've listed the names and addresses and phone numbers of agencies that protect children from abuse. When you contact these people, someone will talk with you and your family about what is happening. If you're in danger, they'll be sure to move you to a safe place.

If you don't have a friend or relative to turn to, ask someone you know and trust: your guidance counselor or teacher, your minister or rabbi, or any adult you feel you can talk to.

If they can't or won't help you—don't give up! Ask someone else, or think about talking to a telephone counselor. Some kids feel comfortable talking to a hot-line counselor because their privacy is protected. Besides Nineline, you can call the Child Abuse Hotline (1-800-422-4453). Both are free services. They don't cost you anything but the courage to take the first step.

CHAPTER 5

Numbing the Pain—Drug and Alcohol Addiction

Her words were so slurred, I could barely understand what she was saying.

"Could you speak up, please?" I asked.

"I said," the girl repeated, this time louder, "I said, I just don't know what to do."

Bit by bit, Louise poured out her story. "Today at school I fell down," she related, "and everyone laughed. I was in gym class, and they thought I was just being a clown. I wasn't—I really couldn't keep my balance."

On the way home, she had stopped at a phone booth and called a local drug treatment program some kids had told her about. "You'd be surprised at how many kids have this problem," she told me defensively; "I'm not the only one." The fifteen-year-old had been angry and upset when she found that she was too young to qualify for the program. "I couldn't believe it. What do they think, that only adults have this problem?" Discouraged, she had hung up the phone. "Nobody wants to help me," she began thinking.

The more she thought about it, the worse she felt. Then Louise did something she always did when she felt depressed. It was something she had come to depend on for the past few years whenever something was bugging her: She took a drink. That's how she dealt with uncomfortable feelings; she "ran away" from them. Some kids drink because they're just plain bored, but most do so because they don't want to face the struggles and conflicts that are a part of everybody's teen years.

Drinking was an easy habit to pick up, even though Louise was a minor and was breaking the law every time she drank. In her small town in northern Michigan she could break into her parents' liquor cabinet or help herself to the beer or wine or hard stuff available at parties. "Everyone else does," she said defensively.

But she wasn't having fun anymore. In the past few months she had had a few "accidents," but nothing like the incident in gym class today. "I could have broken my neck when I fell off the balance beam," she said, starting to cry. "I could have really hurt myself."

"It must have been scary to realize that drinking could have really hurt you," I said.

"I am scared," Louise said. "I don't know what to do. I heard they lock you up in some places. I just want a place I can go in and out of."

"What you really need to do," I suggested, "is to sit down and talk with someone who can help you figure out what's best for you."

"I don't know," Louise said, hesitating.

"There's a hospital near you," I went on, "that has a program for teenagers. How about if I give them a call and see if there's someone there you can talk to?"

"What about my parents? I don't want them to know."

"Let's start by getting some information," I answered. "Sooner or later, though, your folks are going to have to know, and it might help you a lot to have them behind you."

"I don't think so," Louise said again, sounding really miserable this time, "my folks are going to be really mad. You see, they're the reason I began drinking."

She took her first drink when she was barely twelve, the girl said. Her parents fought a lot, and so she did what they did to relax once they finished arguing: She took a drink. Her parents fought constantly, so the next time they fought and Louise couldn't stand the tension —she took a drink. It helped her relax. After a while that was the pattern: Every time her parents argued, Louise drank; that's how she dealt with her anxiety.

Only she couldn't admit that to herself; if she thought about it at all, she blamed her parents. But after this morning, she couldn't keep on doing that. She knew she had to make a change and take a step, however shaky, in the right direction.

Louise's story is not an isolated one, though; drug and alcohol abuse is on the rise among teens and preteens. Because substance use and abuse have a lot of the same motivating reasons and causes in common, I decided to discuss them together.

More than half of all hospitalizations today are drug- and alcohol-related. The list of accidents and illnesses that substance abuse can cause is almost endless. Ironically, a lot of kids say they start using drugs and alcohol because it's a "fun" thing to do.

The alcohol epidemic

Today the average age for a first drink is 12.3 years old—almost the exact age Louise was when she took her first drink.[8] In fact, one in every three teenagers from the ages of fourteen through seventeen has a problem with alcohol.[9]

The pressure to drink, though, starts a few years earlier; according to some experts, as early as four and five years of age when many children become aware of drinking from watching commercials on TV as well as their own parents and begin to mimic their behavior.[10] Between the ages of two and eighteen, in fact, for example, American children see an average of 100,000 beer commercials.[11] By the time children enter the fourth grade they are aware of the pressure to drink and use drugs.[12] Over a third of all fourth-graders say kids their age push them to try beer, wine, or liquor.[13] However, only 50 percent of them know that beer, wine, and liquor are drugs just like marijuana.[14]

Some of this pressure is external, and some of it is internal. We're influenced a lot more than we realize by TV advertising, for instance. Basic aspirin just isn't good enough anymore; now we have "extra strength" pain relief to get rid of a headache fast. We even think that if we use a certain product such as toothpaste or deodorant—or alcohol—we'll get rid of the uncomfortable feelings we have about not fitting in with the crowd and being popular and well liked.

As a result, drinking can become an escape. It's another way of running away from what's bothering you. I think that's what happened to Louise. She didn't have "just a little problem" that was beginning to cause her worries now, at the age of fifteen; her problems had started years earlier as she watched her parents fight and drink.

Not only was Louise afraid to confront her parents, she was also afraid to let go of the drinking. Over the years she had built up a real dependence on alcohol. The drug was a pacifier, the one "friend" she relied on when everything and everybody else let her down. Like many drugs, alcohol had the numbing effect Louise wanted in order to forget what was happening at home.

Yes, I called alcohol a drug. Surprisingly, a lot of kids think of alcohol as a harmless substance. They are wrong: Alcohol can not only hurt you, but, like all drugs, it can even kill you. Let's look at some of the facts.

The risks of alcohol

- Every five seconds a teenager is involved in a drug- and/or alcohol-related accident.
- More than half of all teenage deaths result from drug and/or alcohol abuse.[15]
- Accidents involving drunk drivers are the leading killers of young people between sixteen and twenty-four years old.[16]

How could such a "harmless" substance cause so much abuse?

In its *acute, short-term* phases, alcohol affects every

part of your body as it is absorbed quickly into your bloodstream. It slows down your central nervous system, affects your nerve-muscle functioning, and lessens your ability to think. It also causes depression and fatigue. You may not notice any of these changes, because you feel happy and relaxed and talkative in the first stage of intoxication. The more you drink, though, the more dangerous these stages become. You'll experience:

- uncontrolled behavior and slowed reactions;
- slurred speech;
- inability to stand or walk;
- passing out; breathing may stop at this stage, and you can go into a coma that can result in death.

With *chronic, long-term* alcohol use, the effects become more dangerous: Serious medical complications, including hepatitis, pneumonia, memory blackouts, aggressive behavior, and physical deterioration can result.

These facts should make most kids stop and think before they take a drink. *Use* can lead to an increased *tolerance,* or capacity for more alcohol, which can finally result in *abuse.*

I'm glad Louise decided to pay attention to the "warning sign" of a careless accident that told her she was in trouble and needed help. Other signals include:

- an increased tolerance for alcohol;
- a sense of urgency about drinking;
- becoming drunk more easily and more often;
- starting to shake before you take your first drink, and then experiencing instant relief when you do;
- denial that you have a problem.

If you're addicted to alcohol, you can't really stop on your own. Your body will go into withdrawal if it doesn't have alcohol.

If you do try to stop abruptly, you can hurt yourself. You may feel headachy and dizzy before you get "the sweats" and start shaking and vomiting. Your body is trying to "tell" your brain that it wants alcohol; if you don't listen to those commands you can become seriously ill and go into convulsions and die. "Mind over matter" no longer works. It's "matter over mind" now.

Your body is going through withdrawal; it is being deprived of the one substance it has learned to survive on—and it is fighting back!

Why do kids drink?

Simple: Most kids start drinking because something is bothering them.

If your parents fight, you can drink as a reaction to their problems. You can also develop problems of your own and start drinking as a way out. And sometimes you start drinking just because your friends do, and because you think you'll fit in better and feel better if you do, too.

The problem is that you're probably covering up how you really feel.

If you're taking "just one drink" before a big test at school or before a date, for instance, it's time to stop and think. What you're doing to yourself is building up a tolerance for alcohol. Pretty soon "just one drink" won't be enough to calm you down or cheer you up. You'll need two drinks, then three, then... Do you see what I mean?

Most of all, you're still avoiding what's bothering you.

So don't be fooled: You're not just "using" alcohol—it's using you.

Taking the next step

That's what Louise finally realized when she called.

"So how do you feel now?" I asked her. "How do you feel after having a few drinks to 'calm down'?"

"I'd really like just to keep talking to you," she said after a moment. "I'm glad to hear that," I answered, "and we can talk for the rest of the night if you want to. But there are lots of people like me who can listen to you and help you sort through things. How about if I call the hospital and find someone for you to talk to? Most hospitals now have social workers on staff, and I bet there's one there who can see you right away."

Louise drew a big breath. "All right," she said, sounding relieved. "If I don't get help now, I probably never will, and I'll grow up to be like my folks. I'll go."

Most of the time at Nineline, we don't get a chance to find out what happened to the kids we try to help, but a few days later one of the other counselors waved me over. It was Louise, and she was asking for me. "Hi! Remember me, the girl from Michigan? I just wanted to let you know things turned out okay. They're not perfect," she admitted. "I think it's going to be hard. My parents and I are going to a counselor together, and the program at the hospital isn't easy either, but things are changing. Thanks again for listening to me."

If you're addicted, you need help from someone who understands how to help you deal with your addiction. Your school may have a drug counselor you can talk to. You can also call Alateen, the organization that helps young alcoholics with advice and counseling. We've also listed some additional resources in the Appendix.

The risks of drugs

Like alcohol, drug addiction has reached epidemic proportions among teenagers thirteen to seventeen years old (especially with crack and lately LSD). Many kids begin using drugs to deal with uncomfortable feelings: pressure from friends, parents, and school are some of the big ones. Others start using drugs simply because it makes them feel good or gives them a false sense of security and confidence.

Drug use has differing stages, but use can quickly become abuse, especially if you're a teenager. You can absorb more of everything because of the rate at which your body is growing and changing. It's hard to limit yourself to "just this once." It's a lot like that commercial for potato chips: "Bet you can't eat just one!" The stages of drug abuse are:

1. *Experimentation*—You try drugs once or twice, and usually in a social situation where someone else is providing them.
2. *Occasional Use*—Drug use is still not anything that you anticipate or plan for, and usually it happens in a social setting with others.
3. *Regular use*—At this level, you plan drug use: when you're going to do drugs, where you'll buy them, and how and with whom you're going to use them.
4. *Dependency*—By this time, you are doing drugs

regularly, and very often getting high alone. Use
has become a regular habit, something you plan
to do with regularity and increasing frequency.

The risks of taking the following widely used drugs
are even scarier. The following information comes from
Phoenix House, an excellent drug rehabilitation center
in New York City that helps teenagers and adults alike
kick the drug habit:

Cocaine and crack. This drug can be smoked, sniffed,
or injected, but the consequences are the same: Cocaine
can kill you. "Snorting" (inhaling) the drug can damage
nasal passages; inflammation and ulcerations are also
common, along with a dramatic increase in heart rate
and blood pressure. Smoking cocaine (or crack) is worse,
because it increases the risk of overdose and psychological dependency. Smokers cannot control dosage and
usually increase their intake rapidly. Use of the drug by
injection can produce skin abscesses and other problems
(including AIDS and hepatitis) caused by the use of
equipment that has not been sterilized. Chronic use of
cocaine, regardless of the means of administration, can
produce paranoid delusions, psychosis, and death by
cardiac or respiratory arrest.

Marijuana. This drug has been around for so long—
and seems so "innocent" compared to the powerful
new synthetics available today—that some kids actually
think it can't hurt you. The truth is that this drug distorts
your ability to realize how much it *is* hurting you. In
some tests marijuana use is being shown to cause brain
changes, and some experts are afraid that it may ultimately be proved to cause brain damage.

The marijuana available today is ten to fifteen times

stronger than that available just ten years ago. Heavy pot smokers may seriously damage their lungs, much as heavy cigarette smokers do. Because marijuana smokers inhale a hot unfiltered gas containing powerful irritants and draw the smoke deep into their lungs, the damage may well occur in a relatively short time.

In addition, marijuana smoke contains many of the same cancer-causing agents found in cigarette smoke— some in much larger amounts. THC, the unique chemical substance found in marijuana that is primarily responsible for the drug's mind-altering quality, affects the hormones that regulate the female reproductive system. Marijuana use also lowers the sperm count in males. Studies have shown that marijuana causes the heart to beat faster and work harder, and several studies suggest that the use of marijuana may impair resistance to disease by suppressing the user's immune system.

The most common acute effect is a state of severe anxiety known as "panic reaction." Emergency rooms admit many thousands of victims each year suffering from acute panic induced by marijuana. Although most cases respond favorably to simple reassurance and disappear in a few hours as the drug wears off, many others require professional help. In addition, use of this drug can bring emotional problems to the surface and trigger such severe psychological disorders as schizophrenia. Regular users who smoke marijuana to relieve depression frequently cause the problem to become worse. An estimated 5,000 persons seek professional help *every month* for problems related to marijuana use.

Use of this drug poses a particular hazard for young people. Marijuana use interferes with the normal process of growing up. Young people who use it never learn to address problems in the mature, independent, and responsible way necessary to become healthy adults.

Hallucinogens. A resurgence of hallucinogens has occurred lately; PCP is one of them. Hallucinogens are produced in liquid, powder, tablet, or rock crystal form. Like all such drugs, PCP distorts the perceptions and reality of the person taking it, who acts on the basis of what he or she is feeling. If you feel like flying after you use PCP, you'll try to. If you feel like killing someone, you'll try that too. Death can result from respiratory failure brought on by overdose. In addition, PCP poisoning, which is a real risk because this drug is produced by "basement" chemists, requires psychiatric hospitalization. Multiple seizures, brain hemorrhaging, high fever, and kidney failure can also occur.

Heroin. Addiction is not the only risk taken by users of this drug. A sufficiently large amount of heroin can cause overdose. Users also risk a mysterious fatal reaction that closely resembles overdose. These "heroin-related deaths" are caused by pulmonary edema (flooding of the lungs). The impurities and adulterants found in heroin can also do serious physical damage. Users who inject heroin are susceptible to abscesses, infections, and diseases such as hepatitis, tetanus, and endocarditis (inflammation of the heart lining and valves). What's more, AIDS now has to be counted among the consequences of using heroin.

No drug is harmless! The personal experience of many of the kids who come to Covenant House for help or call the Nineline proves that to me every day. In fact, a drug habit just adds to the problems that they have to struggle with.

Confronting yourself

Are any of the risks we've discussed worth it to you—
worth risking your life? It may take you a long time to
admit that you have a problem, because one of the chief
characteristics of drug abuse is to avoid facing yourself.
Be honest and ask yourself these questions:

- Do I want this drug so much that I plan my days
  around it or can't stop thinking about the next
  time I can have some?
- Am I changing my behavior? Do friends and family
  complain that they "just don't know me anymore"?
  Have I gone from being friendly to withdrawn,
  from quiet to loud?
- Have I changed my friends, especially to new
  ones who endorse my use of drugs as a "fun" or
  "cool" thing to do?
- What am I willing to do to get this drug:
  —steal?
  —lie?
  —cheat?
  —worse?

It's not easy to confront yourself. Don't wait for something serious to happen before you admit you have a
problem that needs attention.

CHAPTER 6

An Urgent
Problem—Crack

Friends and family pleaded with Ed over and over again, but he didn't hear them—he couldn't. He liked doing drugs; he didn't want to stop.

Desperate, Ed's parents were thinking about how they could get their sixteen-year-old son to go into a drug treatment program. Before they could make a decision, though, Ed made his own: He decided to run to the street—"to get away from it all. I couldn't stand their preaching anymore."

Ed thumbed his way to Ft. Lauderdale, where drugs were easy to buy. "For the first few weeks it was like being let loose in a candy store," he told me. "I couldn't get enough—every type of drug you could imagine. The marijuana I had started with was nothing. I'm talking speed, cocaine, LSD." Finally crack hooked him and hooked him hard.

If it was bad before, it got a lot worse now. Crack

addiction is worse than anything you can imagine—a thousand times worse than alcohol or any other drug. Crack consumes you so fast that you don't have time to stop and realize what's happening.

After a few weeks he started "hooking" something else to survive—himself. "I had nothing left after a while," Ed told me. "Sold my radio, my backpack, even my fancy sneakers."

"Then I started dealing. I was hustling (prostituting) to get money for dope and dealing crack to my friends to have money to buy more. I got to the point where I didn't feel nothing." That's one thing crack does, completely wipes you out, numbs you, like novocaine. Nothing else mattered.

Ed moved into a rundown motel near the beach with a bunch of other kids. "The place I was living in was so gross, it didn't even have hot water. One night I decided to take a bath to think things over, but I sat there for a long time in ice-cold water before I realized that I was freezing! My mind was completely blank. I kept trying and trying, but I couldn't remember what I was supposed to be thinking about."

"Finally I got out of the tub and went into the other room. Some kids in the place were 'cracking' it up, really wasting themselves, and as I watched them a feeling came over me that was worse than the chill I got from sitting in the tub. 'My God,' I thought, 'they're killing themselves—and *I'm* responsible. *I* sold them that crack. *I* fed their habits. *I* made them addicts—and *I'm* one myself.' That thought made me go cold. I knew I had to do something, or I was going to end up dead."

Ed was lucky to realize that in time. When he called the Nineline, he was literally only steps away from our shelter in Ft. Lauderdale. Tragically, many young users die before they have a chance to turn their lives around.

All drugs are addictive, but crack is something else. The craving for this drug is so intense that you never can get enough—but it can kill you before you realize that.

Addicted to death: The risks of crack

Crack is a very strong form of cocaine that can be smoked. The drug takes its name from the "crackling" sound you hear when you smoke it. That's because crack is made by cooking cocaine with sodium bicarbonate or other chemicals to make it stronger.

Crack hit the street around 1985, but it isn't a new drug. Freebase cocaine (which is injected for a more intense rush) has been used for many years, and a form of crack known as "rock" has been on the West Coast for several years. As dangerous as cocaine is, it is nothing compared to its smokeable forms.

Why do I call crack dangerous? Why do I consider it the most frightening drug I have seen in almost twenty-five years of experience with kids? Because crack is intensely addictive. It is more addictive than any other drug, including heroin, and it is five to ten times stronger than cocaine. Because crack is smoked instead of sniffed, it travels directly from your lungs to your brain in less than ten seconds—that's why it is so dangerous.

The rush you get is so intense that you want to do it again. The intoxication is far more intense than cocaine—much quicker, much more euphoric, and much, *much* more addictive. That's why kids get hooked on crack so fast. "I'm twenty-four seven," they'll tell you, meaning that they're using crack twenty-four hours a day, seven days a week, even though they just started "cracking" a few weeks or even days ago. They say they can't help it, it feels so good, the rush is so great...

Even though cocaine is ten times as expensive, crack will cost you more if you get hooked because you will need more of it. The first "hit" wears off in fifteen minutes or less, and then you've got to have more right away. At first, you tell yourself it's not too bad, you can afford it. Crack isn't very expensive the first time around—three to four small "rocks" are sold in a vial for $10 to $20.

What starts as an experiment, though, soon turns into a nightmare. The more you use, the more you want, and the more it costs you, and after a while you'll do anything for it. Once you get on the crack merry-go-round, it is hard to get off.

That's where the real tragedy of crack begins: The only way you can afford to go "twenty-four seven" is to make a lot of money. If you're a kid on the street with no place to go, face it, that means selling drugs, stealing— or selling yourself. All of these choices are illegal. They are also very, very dangerous.

Compounded with the other dangers kids face on the street, crack sets off a combustion that consumes you without mercy.

Out on the street

"...10:17 p.m. We drove around Hell's Kitchen where we met Lisa, who had just bought $60 worth of crack and was very high. She talked about how hard it was for her to get into a drug program...

"10:30 p.m. We arrived at—Bar, where there was a

lot of activity. We met Keith, who talked at length about his crack addiction...

"10:55 p.m. We arrived at the Loop and met with many youths. All of them felt like talking and were very descriptive about their feelings and experiences with crack and hustling..."

These words happened to come across my desk as I was thinking about how I could describe the risks of crack to you. I think the kids whose stories you just read describe it a lot better. I took the words from a recent night's log of *off the streets*, the van outreach team at Covenant House that works with homeless and runaway kids on the streets of New York. (We also have outreach teams in other cities where we have shelters, for the simple reason that kids who are on the street often don't know how to get help.)

The big topic of conversation these days out on the street, the one that most concerns the kids besides the threat of AIDS, is crack.

Lisa, for instance, said she wants to get into a drug treatment program—but she won't give up crack. "It's the best friend I ever had," says the eighteen-year-old girl.

Outside a certain bar in midtown Manhattan where young boys sell themselves to survive, Keith told us that crack was how he got started in "the business." He was in a "crack house," a place where you can go and crash while loading up on the drug, when he started selling himself too. "I had to," he said miserably; "I needed more and more money to buy the crack."

Over at "the Loop," on the East Side, crack is big business along with kids hustling themselves. "Crack gets you higher and keeps you going longer," Richie explained defensively. "You can do more business that way."

None of these kids really understood how dangerous crack was before they tried it—and they couldn't stop it once they started. As twenty-year-old Michael told me mournfully, "Nobody wants to go with you because you begin to look like a drug addict. You get tired and worn out and start to look like hell. The combination of turning five or six tricks an hour for five or six hours a night—every night—and taking crack as many times catches up with you after a while."

That's not the worst part of a crack addiction, though. Lots of other bad things can happen. You get caught up in a vicious circle of using and being used, both by the drug and by other people, because you're so desperate to have crack.

Crack and street violence

If you get caught up in crack, you also stand a good chance of getting caught up in the violence that's part of the crack scene. You won't realize that at first, because getting your supplies free will sound like a pretty good deal.

In this case, though, what you don't know *will* hurt you more. Because of the enormous profits involved in selling crack, you'll be putting yourself at enormous risk. Battles for turf among dealers and police raids are common, and often kids are the ones who pay with their lives.

Other kids like Theresa are casualties in the crack war. The seventeen-year-old was a prostitute we knew from our outreach program who started selling herself for crack. She was so desperate for the drug that she was prostituting herself up until the day her baby was born. The girl she gave birth to recently will probably suffer and die because her mother was addicted to crack.

Crack and AIDS

You may already know that two of the ways you can get AIDS are by having sex with someone who has been infected with the AIDS virus, and by shooting drugs yourself.

But knowing is only half of doing.

Lately a lot of these kids are coming to Covenant House for help. Desperate to have crack, they will have sex with drug users in exchange for more crack or sell themselves to a customer to pay for the drug.

By the time they come to us, it's too late for us to help them—these unfortunate kids test positive with the AIDS virus. They were so desperate to have crack that they ignored the facts that could have saved their lives.

A national addiction

You may think you can handle crack, but you're only lying to yourself; *nobody* can handle crack. Every day big-name athletes and celebrities and even Olympic contenders get caught or break down and then finally tell the truth that they are drug addicts. But cocaine addiction doesn't happen just to celebrities. Between 1981 and 1984 cocaine-related deaths more than doubled, and cocaine-related emergency room visits tripled.[17]

Why are we shocked? Cocaine and crack did not emerge from a vacuum. Drug abuse in the United States has climbed at an alarming rate from its emergence twenty years ago as part of the hippie counterculture. Today, drug abuse has become almost respectable for mainstream America, with more people hospitalized for drug addiction than there are beds available for them. Americans now consume a staggering 60 percent of the world's illegal drugs.[18] In every high school graduating class 60 percent of the students have tried drugs.[19]

Taking the next step

According to our own counselors, on any given day at Covenant House 25 to 30 percent of our kids are substance abusers, with the primary drug (at most of our shelters) being crack. Sometimes they have to wait for weeks until a place opens up in a program that can help them deal with their addiction.

To make things even harder on themselves, crack users are often "poly-drug" users, which means that they rely on alcohol and other drugs to enhance the high and relieve the dramatic effects of the crack crash. Some kids even mix cocaine or its derivatives with alcohol or other drugs for an even greater high.

These kids have a really hard time of it, and my heart goes out to them. I guess that's why I believe kids shouldn't even "try" drugs. In my opinion, trying drugs—especially cocaine or crack—is like stepping off the curb into the path of a speeding bus. If someone told you that you should go ahead and take a chance, would you think of that person as a friend? Drugs are just as dangerous. You could be making a choice that will cripple you for the rest of your life.

At the very least, drugs harm you; at the very worst, they can kill you. If something is bothering you, drugs aren't the answer. There are a lot better ways you can learn to feel good about yourself.

CHAPTER 7

Checking Out— Suicide

Only six months ago, the girl said, she was a cheerleader, pretty and popular, and she was a straight-A student, too.

Now she was sitting in a motel room hundreds of miles away from home, the kind of place where nobody knows your name—and nobody cares. She was sitting on a bed holding a razor in her hand and looking at her wrists, she said. "There's no other way," she insisted between heartbreaking sobs. "I don't want this to get better, because it can't."

Those were Cindy's actual words. In a way, I think they shocked me more than the razor I knew she was holding. The utter hopelessness in her voice made me wonder what could possibly have happened to make this seventeen-year-old girl feel so desperate.

I got my answer soon enough. Cindy had run away

from home the night before, she said, "because my father had beaten the heck out of me. But there's more to it to that," she kept saying, while refusing to tell me what "it" was. Finally, as the conversation went on for over two and a half hours, the runaway blurted out the truth: Six months ago her father had started sexually abusing her.

Somehow she had thought she could live with the situation, she said, but as the weeks went by she realized she couldn't live with herself. "I don't want this to get better, because it can't," Cindy kept repeating. She was sure there was nothing else she could do. She didn't think anything could change, she said, but she'd like to talk to me a while before she killed herself. But I started saying a silent prayer for her safety as I kept listening and talking, hoping that somehow I would be able to help her change her mind.

Dangerous myths about suicide

Most suicide calls like Cindy's are literally "calls for help"; the caller wants somebody to know what is happening and is hoping—although feeling terribly scared and confused—that somehow things will change and get better.

Suicide—especially teenage suicide—has a lot of myths surrounding it. By "myths" I mean exaggerated thoughts and ideas that aren't true.

Thinking that someone *doesn't* want help is probably the biggest myth about suicide. Nine out of ten teen suicide attempts happen at home, and 70 percent of them occur between 3 p.m. and midnight, because the

potential suicides are hoping someone will find them—
and stop them.[20]

Some myths about suicide:

*The person who is suicidal can't be stopped; the suicide
can only be delayed.* In a study of people who made
lethal attempts, most intended to die at the time but
later were glad they were alive. Also, most people who
have suicidal thoughts do not wish to die; they only want
the problems or pain to go away, and they can't think of
any other options.

Asking about suicide can "plant" the idea. Don't be
afraid to ask! Your concern can lower someone's anxiety
about dealing with his or her feelings.

Suicidal people are mentally ill. Only about 25 percent
of suicidal people are psychotic. The rest are relatively
normal people in the midst of an overwhelming crisis.

Suicidal people haven't received enough love. All kinds
of people commit suicide, including people who are
depressed because of biochemical factors that have
nothing to do with love.

Every suicide attempt is a serious effort to die. Some
people *do* want to die; most, however, are desperately
trying to get help in order *not* to die. The final act
usually happens after a long period of stress or depression during which the person has been trying to tell
other people how they are feeling and has been ignored.
This is especially true with teenagers, who some people
think are depressed a lot of the time or exaggerate how
they feel to get attention.

People who threaten suicide won't really go through

with it. Many people do; they often talk about killing themselves before they do.

People who attempt suicide are just trying to get attention. A suicide attempt is a desperate cry for help—if it's ignored, the consequences can be fatal.

Everyone needs to pay more attention to the risks of teenage suicide. Adults do, and you should, too, so you can help your friends who are in trouble. According to a recent National Adolescent Student Health questionnaire, as many as one in every seven teenagers may have attempted suicide.[21] The suicide rate among teenagers has tripled since 1950. That means that this year nearly 6,000 high school kids will commit suicide—but that does not include the nearly 400,000 who will attempt it or try it again. And the real tragedy is that most of these kids are average kids.

Knowing the warning signs

Cindy was exactly that type of kid: a straight-A student who was active and involved in lots of activities at school. As her father kept up his abusive behavior, though, Cindy changed hers: She quit cheerleading squad, her grades went down, she stopped dating, and she got careless and sloppy about her appearance.

Someone should have noticed. Cindy was trying to "tell" people through her actions that something was wrong, even though she didn't put her feelings into words. She was too embarrassed and humiliated by what was happening to talk to anyone.

To make matters worse, every time people tried to get close Cindy pushed them away and started lying to cover up the truth. After a while, if people don't think you want help, they don't offer. Unfortunately, that only increased her isolation and loneliness. Cindy decided that the only way she could solve her problem was to kill herself.

Whether they are verbalized or not, "warning signs" like Cindy's should be listened to and responded to. *Pay attention to:*

- a loss of interest in personal appearance;
- an increase in the use of drugs or alcohol;
- a loss of interest in hobbies, work, school;
- direct talk about suicide or indirect hints: "Life's not worth it," "People would be better off without me," or "There's no sense going on";
- drastic actions like giving away possessions, changing eating or sleeping habits, withdrawing from friends, going around to friends to "tie up loose ends," making a will;
- communication problems with parents;
- suicide of a relative or close friend;
- absence of one or both natural parents through death, divorce, or separation;
- conflicts with stepparents;
- recent severe illness of a family member that has obliged the teenager to take on adult responsibilities.

Sometimes it's hard to ask for help, but a suicide attempt isn't the way to get it.

That's what Cindy realized as she sat in that hotel

room with a razor in her hand. Her feelings had scared her so much that she ran away from them. When she got to the motel she realized she hadn't left them behind. She was sure there was only one solution left that could give her peace of mind, but fortunately she decided to make one last call.

"A permanent solution"

"I don't want this to get better," Cindy told me, "because it can't."

The hopelessness in her voice alarmed me. Most suicidal callers are just thinking about taking that final step. She had already made up her mind.

"It sounds as if you've thought a lot about this," I said.

"Yes, I have," Cindy said calmly. "I want to end my life. I want this to be over. I'm sick of thinking about it."

"It sounds as if you've been through a lot in the past few months," I said.

The teenager didn't say anything for a minute. Then, "Everything changed."

"Do you want to talk about it?" I asked.'

"No, I don't," she answered. "There's more to it than that. But I don't want to talk about it. It's over."

"Sounds to me as if you have a lot going for you," I continued, "cheerleading, lots of activities, good grades."

"That's all in the past," the girl said, suddenly bitter. "It's over."

"Things seem really rough for you right now," I said. "Sometimes, when you're feeling down, it's hard to remember that it can get better."

"There's more to it than that," she repeated. "But I

don't want to talk about it. I just want to end my life."

"Are you really sure?" I asked. "Is that what you really want?"

"I can't look at myself in the mirror, don't you understand?" she struggled to control herself but started crying. "My father was having sex with me," she said, her voice breaking, "don't you understand? He took everything from me." The pent-up frustrations and fears of six long months finally exploded.

"It's okay," I said, "you have a right to be angry."

"I don't know," she said, sobbing harder now, "he said he did it because I was bad, I was no good."

"No one deserves to be treated that way," I said.

"How do you know? You don't know me."

"I know that all kids have a right to be loved and protected," I said. "And I know that nobody deserves to be abused. Don't you want things to get better?" I asked.

"They can't," Cindy said. "I can't go home again. So I'm going to end them."

"There are other things you can do," I said. "There's probably a hospital nearby, and lots of them have a counselor you can talk to about this."

"Listen," she said, her voice still shaking, "I really appreciate your help, but I told you, I've made up my mind." Cindy hung up the phone abruptly.

I felt angry and upset at myself. After holding on to her for over two hours, I had lost her—just like that. Sometimes it's hard not to blame yourself. I couldn't stop wondering what had happened to her. Where was she, and was she okay? Or had she...I couldn't even finish my thought.

Twenty-four hours later Cindy called back and asked

to talk to me. She had changed her mind about killing herself, she said. "I looked in the mirror one last time," she related, "and I don't know, something stopped me. I remembered what you said about not deserving to be abused. Somehow I wanted to believe that."

"I'm so glad to hear that," I said. "I really am."

"Me, too," said Cindy. "It took a lot to believe that, but your encouragement really helped. I'm ready to talk to someone at that hospital now if you can still find them." Within minutes Cindy was on her way to the hospital to see a social worker named Margaret who would be able to talk to her.

All across this country, there's a network of people like Margaret who care about what happens to kids. You don't have to feel alone and desperate, no matter how bad things are. There are people who are ready and willing to help you if you take the first step by asking for help. They're experts, in particular, at helping you face the uncomfortable and hurtful feelings that are part of a crisis.

Professional help is important, but anyone can learn how to be a part of the process of helping someone who is hurting. Most of our counselors on Nineline, in fact, are volunteers who have learned how to listen to kids like Cindy.

If you know someone who is struggling with these feelings, you can learn to be helpful too. If your friend is really depressed—to the point where he or she has spoken of suicide—take it seriously! Your friend is telling you *exactly* how he or she feels—crying out for help.

Much as you're willing to help your friend, though, your support is not enough. It's also important to realize that ultimately you are not responsible for saving a friend's life.

Someone who knows how to help effectively is needed. Don't feel that you're betraying a friend by letting someone else—a teacher or a counselor at school—know what's happening.

The important thing, as a friend, is to be there when the going gets tough and to let your friend know you care. Your help may make the difference in whether or not someone's "cry for help" is heard and answered.

CHAPTER 8

Caving In—

Peer Pressure

"Why were they so mean to me?" fifteen-year-old Susan asked. "When somebody invites you to a party you're supposed to have a good time. They locked me a room with this boy and said I had to have sex with him before they would let me out. If that's what everyone at my new school is like, I'm not going to have any friends for the next three years."

"I want to know," Larry asked me very seriously. "Can you get AIDS from kissing someone?"

"I didn't want to have sex with my boyfriend, but he told me he would break up with me if we didn't," sixteen-year-old Candy told me, sobbing. "And now I'm pregnant. What do I do—and how can I tell my parents?"

If I asked you what those stories have in common, what would you say?

You might say that, despite their different circumstances, they all have sex in common.

To a degree, that's true. Decisions about sex are a big part of growing up. But the struggles Susan, Larry, and Candy were facing were not only about sex; they were symptoms of a larger issue called "peer pressure."

Their friends were giving them a hard time for not going along. I bet that sounds familiar to you.

Being part of a group and feeling accepted is important for everyone, especially teenagers. Sharing our thoughts and feelings with others who are going through the same experiences can be one of the best things about growing up. It's a relief to know that somebody besides you has some of the same questions and concerns about—well, everything: how your body is changing, whether or not you'll go to the prom, and how you can go from feeling like leaping tall buildings one day to being down in the dumps the next.

Sometimes you just have to talk with people your own age. They can understand what's really happening with you because often they're having the same struggles.

But sometimes things can get out of hand. Your best friends can start putting you down and making you feel bad if you won't go along with them. That's when peer pressure goes from being positive to negative.

Learning to think for yourself and make your own decisions may be one of the most difficult parts of growing up.

Much as we all want to be popular and liked, it's more important to like yourself. Sometimes going along with the crowd can really hurt you. That's what Susan finally realized.

Listening in

"Is there something wrong with me?" Susan kept asking as she told me her story. "Am I a dud because I didn't want to drink till I threw up or have sex with someone I didn't know? I haven't even had sex yet," she told me, starting to cry, "but when I do, it will sure be with someone I know and love."

"I think your reactions are perfectly normal," I said. "It sounds to me as if you're a little scared about fitting in at this new school."

"Well, yeah, I am," Susan said honestly. "It was a big change, moving here—from a small town down South to a city up North. It's a lot different—everything's faster," she said.

"Including the kids, it sounds like," I said.

"Yes," she said, sounding miserable. "Only now I don't have any friends. If all the parties up here are like that one," Susan told me, trying to joke, "then I guess I'll stay home for the rest of high school."

"But would you call people who wanted you to do things you didn't want to do real friends?" I asked.

Susan hesitated. "What if everyone else at this school is like them?" she asked.

"I don't think that can be true," I said. "Have you gotten to know any other kids?"

"Not really," Susan said. "We've only been up here for a few weeks."

"How about getting involved in activities at school?" I asked.

"Susan said, "I've been too busy helping Mom fix things up at home."

"Sounds as if you haven't really gotten to know anyone

yet, except for that bunch," I said. "I bet if you looked around you'd find some kids you'd like. How about reaching out to them? There may even be some new kids who feel just like you. And can you talk to your mom?"

"She's so busy, I didn't want to bother her," Susan said. "I wanted to try to figure this out on my own. The thing I'm having a hard time understanding is why they were so awful to me."

"I don't think it's you," I said.

"I don't understand," Susan said. "What do you mean?"

"I think the real issue was power—peer pressure. You're the new kid at school, so they picked on you. I bet they've done that to other kids."

"But why?" Susan said. "I just don't get it."

"Because some kids like to play pranks," I said.

"That doesn't seem very funny to me," Susan said.

"Unfortunately, some kids don't think about how they're going to hurt someone. I don't think they meant to hurt you. They just thought they were playing a practical joke."

"But why am I the joke?"

"Simply because you're the new kid. They were testing you to see if you really want to be a member of their group. And it sounds to me as if you're not very comfortable in their type of party situation."

"No way," said Susan. "I don't think you have to drink that much to have fun or joke about sex just to be cool."

"Sounds to me as if you just made a good decision. I think maybe you already knew that," I said.

"I do feel a lot better," Susan said. "And I'm going talk to Mom, too. I've been afraid to bother her, she's been so busy."

"You may be surprised," I said. "I bet she already knows. She's probably just waiting for you to say something."

"Thanks," Susan said, "I'm feeling like my old self again."

Once she talked things out with someone, Susan was able to clear up her confusion and come to some good decisions about what to do. That's especially important when the pressure you're facing from peers involves sexual issues that can hurt or even kill you.

Risking your life

The other day a teenager named Larry called me.

"I have a very important question to ask," the young caller told me seriously. "I just kissed someone, and, um..." He couldn't finish his sentence, he was so nervous.

"Go on, please," I urged him.

"I think maybe you'll think my question is stupid," he said.

"No question is stupid if it's bothering you," I told him. "If it's important enough to bother you, it's important enough for you to bother us."

"I have to know," Larry finally blurted out, "can I get AIDS from kissing someone?"

I wanted to say, "Larry, *everyone* knows you can't get AIDS from kissing someone. That's silly."

Then I stopped and thought a moment—do they? Do *you*, for instance, know the facts about AIDS? Or about how you can be exposed to syphilis or gonorrhea or become pregnant? It's normal to be scared about things we don't understand, but you can find out the facts and make wise decisions instead. You owe it to yourself. Being uninformed or ignorant about sex today can hurt you very badly—and it may even kill you.

So sharpen your pencil and take the following test. There is evidence that AIDS is spread by:

- toilet seats, bathtubs, and showers;
- handshakes or other nonsexual physical contact;
- dishes, utensils, or food handled by a person with AIDS;
- doorknobs, linens, clothing, or other articles touched by a person with AIDS;
- sneezing, coughing, or spitting;
- being around a person with AIDS, even if the contact is daily.

It may surprise you to know that the answer to all of the above is no!

The AIDS virus is not communicated like chicken pox, or the flu, or the common cold, which you can get from other people by talking or sharing a soda or holding hands or kissing. Even family members who have intimate nonsexual contact with a brother or sister or parent who has AIDS don't get infected.

So how do you get AIDS? Does it happen to some people and not to others? Do only homosexuals get AIDS? Or drug users? Should you never give or receive blood because you may get infected?

The truth about AIDS

Most people are not at risk of getting AIDS. You can get AIDS only if you:

- share needles that are infected with the AIDS virus to inject drugs;
- have sexual contact with an infected person;
- are born to a mother who has the AIDS virus;
- had a blood transfusion before tests for AIDS were available.

I think you can see from these facts that AIDS is really very hard to get. So that's the good news. If you're not already infected, you *can* choose to stay that way—by simply avoiding the risks.

Tragically, some kids don't. For some reason, they don't believe they can get AIDS, even though they keep taking the risks that expose them to the virus. They choose to ignore the fact, for instance, that the AIDS virus can stay in your system for years before it appears and begins to make you sick.

The problem is that by then it is too late to do anything about it. You can't get rid of AIDS once you have it. Unlike an addiction to drugs or alcohol, where you can make things change if you are willing to try very hard, you can't change or stop the progress of this terrible disease. So far there is no vaccine and no cure.

We've had dozens of street kids come to Covenant House for help in the past few months—and I'm afraid there will be many more in the next few years. And the sad, sad truth is that it will be too late for most of them.

When Robert first walked into our clinic, he complained about feeling tired and run down. One of the things about AIDS is that in its initial stages it can look like a lot of other illnesses. But a few weeks later Robert wasn't feeling any better. In fact, the seventeen-year-old was feeling a lot worse. We knew something was wrong, but we didn't know what until he contracted pneumonia, and we had to put him in the hospital. By then, of course, we knew he had AIDS.

And he knew, too, even though he was in so much pain that he could hardly move. It was always hard not to cry, because you knew he was dying—and there was nothing you could do to save him.

Have you ever seen someone die of AIDS? I have, and I hope you never do. It is a slow and painful death. By the time Robert died, he looked like a skeleton. After a while he had to have a tube stuck down his throat for feeding because he couldn't swallow. The last forty-eight hours of his life were spent hooked up to life support machines so he could breathe. And then he had a massive heart attack and died.

He wasn't even eighteen years old. His life was over before it really had a chance to begin. Because he made the mistake, one desperate night, of having sex with a drug user who was infected.

How not to get AIDS

Robert didn't believe he could get sick and die. Somehow he thought he could expose himself to the risks and not contract AIDS.

Maybe you believe that too. You may be thinking, "That could never happen to me. I'm not a street kid. I don't have sex with drug users or use needles—so I don't have to worry."

But maybe you are sexually active. Do you realize that you, too, may be putting yourself at deadly risk—just like Robert?

Perhaps you didn't know that the AIDS virus can be

passed from partner to partner through sexual inter-course—even if you have sex just once or with just one partner. If you or your partner is sexually active, though, the risk of getting AIDS actually multiplies. That's because AIDS is spread through direct blood-to-blood or semen-to-blood contact. If you want to avoid the risk of getting it, it's pretty easy to figure out what you have to do: Don't shoot drugs and don't have sex with people who you are not 100 percent sure aren't infected. But my best advice—if you want to *absolutely* protect your-self from getting AIDS—is to abstain from sex until you are married. It works, and it could save your life.

The risk of young love

"My boyfriend wants me to have sex with him—what should I do?"

"I only had sex once—I can't get pregnant, right?"

Sometimes the conversations are long, and sometimes they are short, but usually one thing happens by the end of every call. The young callers realize that they're just not ready for the commitment that sex and marriage demand.

In another time and place their story might have sounded like Shakespeare's *Romeo and Juliet*, but it wasn't romantic at all. Sixteen-year-old Candy was preg-nant and living with her seventeen-year-old boyfriend in an abandoned warehouse because her parents didn't like her boyfriend. They wanted us to help them figure out how and where they could get married, because they were both minors.

"Do you really want to get married?" I asked.

Candy started crying when she heard that.

"Well," she said, "not really. But I guess we should."

"That's not a good reason for getting married," I told her. "It sounds to me as if you haven't had a chance to think things through."

Candy hesitated. "Yeah, we did rush things," she said defensively, "but so what? We love each other. And what's wrong with being young?"

"Being young isn't the problem," I answered. "Being ready and responsible is." A million and one concerns came to mind. What was she going to do—raise the baby in a warehouse? I wondered if she had thought about the hospital, or even had any prenatal care. The statistics on infant mortality among young girls who give birth to underweight babies because they don't have regular medical care are truly frightening.[22] And last—but not least—what were they going to do about money? A future without at least a high school degree is nothing to look forward to.

Candy must have been reading my mind. "What am I going to do?" she asked.

"Well," I said, "the first thing is, you can't stay in that warehouse. There are probably rats and who knows what all else. You've got to go someplace safe. I'd recommend a shelter, particularly a place where you can begin to get medical care and also some counseling about some of the decisions you have to make."

"I already know one," Candy said firmly. "I want to keep my baby; I don't want an abortion. Nobody's going to change my mind about that." After talking for a while, Candy decided to go to Birthright, an organization that will help her do just that. We were able to put her in contact with one of the counselors.

"I know it's not going to be easy, but I feel okay," she said. "And who knows, maybe in a while my folks and I can talk again. I learned it the hard way, but I guess that's what growing up means—taking responsibility for your own decisions."

CHAPTER 9

How to Be Your Own Best Friend

School. Friends. Dating. Sex. Parents. *Pressure.* Sometimes it all gets to be too much. It seems as if you have one big decision after another to face when you're growing up.

What do you do? How do you make good decisions—especially when things get really tense and it's hard to think clearly?

Number one, give yourself a break. You've heard the saying, "Rome wasn't built in a day." Same goes for growing up.

Not that you should always, as a rule, put off till tomorrow what you should or could do today. Don't procrastinate if you can do it now. Most of the time, thinking about making a decision can be a lot worse than actually making it. That's especially true if you're facing a serious decision where a delay in getting help can really hurt you.

The problem can seem so overwhelming that you don't know where to start. The more you think that way, though, the worse things will look. What you need to do instead is to figure out what steps to take to solve your problem. I call these steps "strategies" because you will need patience and persistence in finding a way around the obstacles to a successful solution.

How to Communicate

Being young does put you low on the totem pole of power—but you are not helpless. Try these tactics when you're facing a tough situation with friends, teachers, or parents:

1. Use your head to figure out what the other person is thinking. Then talk to that person in a way he or she can understand.
2. Don't accuse or criticize the other person. That will force him or her to stick up for himself—and pick on you all over again.
3. Stick to the facts and say how you feel about them. If you're angry, that's okay, but try not to lose your temper. Don't name-call.
4. Practice what you want to say with another friend first; this will help you anticipate possible comments and objections and prepare a reply.
5. It's no help to win the argument if the problem is still unresolved. Think about how you can compromise so that you and the other person can come to a solution you both can live with.

We've discussed family conflicts and abuse at home in

previous chapters, but I'm going to repeat some of the earlier information here and then expand on it.

PARENTS

Parents who nag or criticize

- Keep your parents on your side by showing love, appreciation, and interest in them and by being as pleasant to them as you want them to be to you.
- Ask for details about what's bothering them—and then listen. That gives you time to think things through.
- Show that you've listened and understood by repeating what they have said. Then bring up what's bothering you again.
- Get them to talk about what they did as teenagers—it may remind them of how they felt.

Parents who are overprotective

- Parents usually make rules because they love you and don't want you to be hurt. Show them that you understand the dangers they fear.
- Statements like, "Everyone else is allowed to," "It's my life," "Times have changed," didn't work for your parents—and they won't work for you.
- Keep them up-to-date on your life. Let them meet your friends and see where you hang out.
- Think up options you think are fairer than theirs, and ask your parents to try them.
- Get a friend's parents to talk to them about how they set rules their kids could live with.
- Write a letter letting them know how you feel.

Parents who fight

- Tell them it upsets you (but not during a fight).
- Get a family friend or relative to step in.
- Try to understand each one's point of view, but don't take sides.
- Go for a walk, phone a friend, or do something else to help you through their fight.

Divorce

- Keep in mind that it's not your fault in any way; it's their relationship that has fallen apart.
- You can't keep it from happening; thinking you can will only make you feel worse.
- Don't let one parent put down the other in front of you. Remind them that you don't have to hate one to love the other.
- Tell the parent you visit that you want to come and visit a lot.
- Focus on your own life. Stay busy with school, friends, and other activities.

A parent's remarriage

- Let your stepparent spend time with your parent. They are in love and need time alone together. Let them know you understand, and don't force your parent to choose between you and a new spouse. Both will be grateful—and nicer to you as a result.
- If you feel left out, talk to your parent and try to reach a compromise.

- Do something nice for your stepparent to break the ice.
- Try to treat your stepparent the way you treat your best friend's parents.
- Ask your parent to set aside a special time for just the two of you.

A parent's problem with drugs or alcohol

- Ask your parent to get help, but don't go it alone. Ask an adult you trust to step in. Call Alateen, a group for other kids in the same boat, or Alanon, a group for families of people with drinking problems.
- Don't let your parent blame you for the problem.
- Remember that your parent's mood swings are a result of the illness. You're not to blame for the problem.

A parent who abuses you physically or sexually

- Tell someone right away—an adult you can trust. If that person doesn't help, tell someone else until you do get help.
- Remember that no parent, stepparent, relative, or friend of the family has the right to abuse you. You are not to blame when someone abuses you. That person's behavior is wrong and not related to anything you did. Don't feel bad for protecting yourself.

FRIENDS

Pressure from friends to drink or do drugs

- Your true friends will go along with your decision. They don't expect you to agree with everything they do.
- If your friends feel that you're putting them down, they may want to put you down, too, and give you a hard time. Try telling them one at a time so that you're not taking on the whole crowd by yourself. You could say things like, "I don't feel like it right now," "Sorry, that stuff really makes me sick," or "I can't get high; I really want to study to pass this test." The trick is to let them know how you feel instead of sounding as if you're criticizing them.
- Stick to your guns. Some people will give you a hard time about your choices. Let them. The consequences of going along could be harder to deal with than saying no.
- Seek out positive activities that make you feel good about yourself, like sports or activities at school or volunteer work.

Pressure about sex

- Remember that having sex won't turn you into a man or a woman—but it might make you pregnant or give you VD or AIDS, even if you do it just once. So consider the risks and be responsible.
- Remember that some kids will brag that they've done "it" when they really haven't just to impress you.

• Don't confuse your desire to please your friend with what is comfortable and right for you. Sex is a very special decision that you shouldn't rush into.

SCHOOL

Bad grades

• What matters is that you try. Maybe you need help in learning to use your time better and to study more effectively, for instance.
• Ask your teacher for help. If you do badly on a test, ask the teacher whether you can work on an extra project to bring up your grades.

Daydreaming and difficulty concentrating

• Are you eating and sleeping enough? Are you skipping breakfast and downing a can of soda before you run off to school in the morning? Too little sleep and too much junk food can lead to feeling run down and unable to concentrate.
• Is something bothering you? If so, find someone you feel comfortable talking to. Try your parents, relatives, a teacher, coach, counselor, a friend's parent.
• If these efforts fail, ask your parent to let you see the doctor. Your inability to concentrate might have biochemical causes.

Falling behind

- Remember, this doesn't mean you're bad or stupid. Maybe you're expecting too much of yourself. Set reasonable goals.
- Try to figure out what the problem is: Is the class too advanced? Is something going on outside of school that is distracting you? Talk to your parents or teacher and come up with a solution.
- Above all, stay in school! Your education is your future. It deserves everyone's best effort, so keep looking for help if you're having a problem.

ANXIETY

Worrying about what people think

- Don't. It doesn't help. We all have things about ourselves we don't like. Talking to your friends or family can help you put things in perspective. Accept the fact that we all feel lonely and inadequate at times; it is part of being human.

Being nervous about doing something

- Try it anyway. A lot of things get easier with practice. Think back to first grade and how hard it was to learn to write your name—now it's a snap. Remember that you learned to write with practice and by taking small steps at a time. The same is true for swimming, talking to groups, going on a blind date, or asking someone out. Also think about seeking out an expert in an activity you would like to try and ask for some advice on how he or she learned to excel.

Upsetting situations

- Think about whether you are seeing the problem fairly. Try out another person's point of view and figure out how that person would feel in the same situation.
- Talk things over with a good friend.
- Put your feelings in writing, in a letter or your diary. (If you don't have a diary, start one. Write in it whenever you have something to say.)
- Do something physical, like jog. Or try some relaxation exercises.
- If you've tried hard to cope and still can't, get help in thinking it through. Sometimes getting out of the situation is the best solution. Big exception: Your family. It will always be important for you to come to terms with your family. If your sincere efforts at communicating don't work, don't give up. If you and your family have serious problems, you may need outside help.

Epilogue—One Last Word

*"It was the best of times,
it was the worst of times,
it was the age of wisdom,
it was the age of foolishness...
it was the season of Light,
it was the season of Darkness,
it was the spring of hope,
it was the winter of despair."*

One of my favorite authors is Charles Dickens, who wrote these words in his novel *A Tale of Two Cities*. To me, they sum up the best and the worst of being a teenager; I like to think of them, in fact, as *The Teenager's Tale of Two Lives* because sometimes that's exactly what growing up seems like. Your teen years truly are the best and the worst of times, the season of light and the season of darkness.

At Nineline we try to help kids who are feeling frustrated and confused about these in-between times they find themselves in. Most kids, fortunately, just need a sympathetic ear and a little help to survive—and thrive—on the ups and downs that are part of growing up. They learn how to make decisions and move through the trying times that mature their character and get them ready for adulthood.

Some kids, though, are not that fortunate. They struggle through childhood and adolescence with enormous problems beyond their control that leave them frightened, insecure, and unable to take the next step. We're especially glad at Nineline to have the opportunity to reach out to these kids. We are here for them, and so are a lot of other caring people whose names and addresses are listed in the back of this book. There are people all across this country who are ready and willing and able, *right now*, to help you if you reach out to them.

It has been my privilege, time and again, to be there for the thousands of kids who needed someone to listen to them and to share their struggles. This has given me an understanding beyond books about what it takes to really help kids.

When you come to the last chapter of a book, the author usually thanks the people who helped write it. A team of people contributed to this book, especially my staff and the volunteers at Nineline. Without them and their commitment to kids, this book, like our twenty-four-hour hotline at Covenant House, would not be able to be there for the thousands of kids who need to reach us.

But another group of people have been even more important to the making of this book, the truly amazing young people who have shared their joys and sorrows with me for over twenty-five years and whose honesty and openness have helped me, in turn, to help thousands of kids. As the saying goes, I have received much more than I have given.

Thank-yous
from Kids

Lenore,
John called to thank you for helping him two months ago. His father accepted him.

Tom,
Barry is home and everything is fine.

To the crisis worker who spoke with Jennifer on Saturday,
She called to say thank you and to let you know that things have worked out well for her.

Mark,
The person you spoke to last night who had attempted to commit suicide called to thank you and say he would definitely get help.

Michele,
Ellen called. She is going to live with her aunt and uncle. They say if they had known what was going on, they would have come to get her when she was nine.

Tracy,
Darlene called. She wanted you to know that her daughter returned home.

To the crisis worker who spoke to Samantha,
She said she wanted to thank the person who talked to her about her runaway friend. They found her and she is okay.

John,
Amanda called. She took your advice to speak to her friend about suspected abuse. She said she feels much closer to her friend now, and she gave her the Nineline number. Thinks she'll call.

Sandy,
Margaret called to say that her father has begun to go to AA meetings and that things will probably get better.

Victor called to say he is home again and thanks to the crisis worker who helped him.

Virginia,
Jim called. He wanted to let you know that things were better with his parents, and that they were communicating better.

To all at Nineline,
Jeff wants to thank everyone. He said that everyone has helped him get himself together. Said if it weren't for Nineline he'd still be out on the streets.

To the man who helped Kathleen return to Texas,
Her dad is greatly appreciative.

Barbara,
Tom called and said thank you. He is at the shelter and it is a nice place.

Liz says thank you, I'm at home trying to work things out.

Peggy,
Steve from Georgia called to tell you that he spoke to his pastor and everything is okay now. He is not thinking about leaving home.

Barbara,
The eleven-year-old boy abandoned in Chicago by his aunt wanted to let you know that he returned to his home in California.

To whoever helped Anne on Sunday and Tuesday last week,
She's doing better. Her mother is treating her better and spoke to a guidance counselor, who's been helping them.

Mike,
Sheila called to say thanks. She went to a referral you gave and says she "got my head straightened out."

Notes

1. "Annual Report to Congress," Runaway and Homeless Youth Program. 1987, U.S. Department of Health and Human Services, p. 1, Washington, D.C.
2. Ann V. Bollinger. "Crack Has Hordes of Teenage Hookers on Streets of New York." New York *Post*, September 6, 1988, p. 4.
3. "Fact Sheet, Runaway and Homeless Youth Program." Washington, D.C.: Family and Youth Services Bureau, 1987.
4. J. Garbarino, J. Wilson, and A.C. Garbarino. "The Adolescent Runaway," in J. Garbarino, C. Schellenback, and J. Sebes, *Troubled Youth, Troubled Families*. New York: Aldine Publishers, 1986.
5. "Fact Sheet, Runaway and Homeless Youth Program." Washington, D.C.: Family and Youth Services Bureau, 1987.
6. Rachel L. Strocof, M.P.H.; Lloyd F. Novick, M.D.; James T. Kennedy, M.D.; Isaac B. Weisfuse, M.D. *Seroprevalence of Antibodies to Human Immunodeficiency of Virus −1 in a Facility for Runaway or Homeless Adolescents in New York City*. American Public Health Association, 116th Annual Meeting, November 14, 1988, Boston, Mass.
7. *To Whom Do They Belong? A Profile of America's Runaway and Homeless Youth and the Programs That Help Them*. Washington, D.C.: National Network of Runaway and Youth Services, July 1987.
8. Nancy P. Gordon and Alfred McAlister. "Promoting Adoles-

cent Health," in *Adolescent Drinking: Issues and Research.* New York: Academic Press, 1982.

9. *NIAAA, Sixth Special Report to the U.S. Congress on Alcohol and Health from the Secretary of Health and Human Services.* Washington, D.C.: DHSS Publication No. (ADM) 281-85-0009, 1987.

10. Ronald D. Adams, consultant, National Parents' Resource Institute for Drug Education, Atlanta, Ga.

11. N. Postman, et al. *Myths, Men and Beer: An Analysis of Beer Commercials on Broadcast Television.* Falls Church, Va.: AAA Foundation for Traffic Safety, 1987.

12. National High School Senior Survey, National Institute of Drug Abuse (conducted by the University of Michigan), 1987.

13. *Weekly Reader National Survey on Drugs and Drinking.* Middletown, Conn.: Field Publications, 1987.

14. *Ibid.*

15. "Drug Abuse: Family Enemy Number One." Springfield, Mo.: National Federation of Parents for Drug-free Youth.

16. *Fact Sheet: National PTA Drug and Alcohol Abuse Prevention Project.* Chicago, National PTA, 1986.

17. *Drug Abuse Warning Network.* Rockville, Md.: National Institute of Drug Abuse, 1987.

18. "America on Drugs." *U.S. News & World Report*, July 28, 1986.

19. Calvin Chatlos, M.D. "Getting Crack Out of Your Town," in *Crack: What You Should Know About the Cocaine Epidemic.* Perigee Books/The Putnum Publishing Group, 1986.

20. Michael Nadlman. "On Teen Suicide." *Teen Line News*, Cedar-Sinai Medical Center, Los Angeles, Calif., Winter, 1988.

21. *National Adolescent Student Health Questionnaire.* American School Health Association, Association for the Advancement of Health Education, and Society for Public Health Information. Conducted by IOX Associates, Los Angeles, Calif., August, 1988.

22. *Advance Report of Final Natality Statistics, Table 15.* Hyattsville, Md., National Center for Health Statistics, 1988.

Appendix

Covenant House Nineline

1-800-999-9999

24 hours a day, 7 days a week, any youth or parent can call the Nineline free, from anywhere in the country, and speak with a trained crisis counselor who will help sort out the problem, look at solutions and provide information and referrals for shelter or additional help in any state.

Nineline also helps teens contact Covenant House shelters where homeless and runaway youth can receive emergency shelter, food, clothing, health care and counseling. At some of our shelters, an outreach van works with teens on the streets. Covenant House programs also provide services for young mothers and their children, and youth in need of educational and vocational counseling and transitional living programs.

Covenant House New York
460 West 41st Street
New York, NY 10036
(212) 613-0300

Covenant House Florida
733 Breakers Avenue
Fort Lauderdale, FL 33304
(305) 561-5559

Covenant House Texas
1111 Lovett Boulevard
Houston, TX 77006
(713) 523-2231

Covenant House New Orleans
613 North Rampart Street
New Orleans, LA 70122
(504) 584-1108

Covenant House Alaska
609 F Street
Anchorage, AK 99501
(907) 272-1255

Covenant House Canada
70 Gerrard Street East
Toronto, Ontario
Canada M5B 1G6
(416) 593-4849

Operation Home Free

Runaway youth ages 12 to 17 can receive transportation home through this Greyhound-Trailways program jointly sponsored by the International Association of Chiefs of Police and Police Chiefs in major cities.

To use the program, a runaway must go to the local police department. The police will confirm that the youth is a runaway (the parent must report the child as such) and find out the bus schedule.

The police will let the family know of the child's arrival time, will accompany the child to the bus terminal just before departure time, and will fill out the necessary form so that Greyhound/Trailways will issue a non-refundable ticket for the youth.

National Hotlines

Child Abuse and Domestic Violence

Child Help USA
(Child Abuse Hotline)   1-800-422-4453
Child abuse hotline providing crisis counseling for abused

youth and for parents involved in child abuse situations; offers referrals to local programs and help in reporting abuse to state agencies.

National Council on Child Abuse
and Family Violence   1-800-222-2000
  in California
Provides information on child abuse and other types of family violence and referrals.

Parents Anonymous   1-800-421-0353
  in California   1-800-352-0386
Provides referrals to local self-help group for abusive parents or those who fear they will do so.

National Domestic Violence Hotline
(Shelter Aid)   1-800-333-SAFE
Provides referrals to people of any age who are victims of domestic violence.

Missing Youth

National Center for Missing
and Exploited Youth   1-800-843-5678
  in Washington, D.C.   634-9836
A clearinghouse for information on missing and exploited youth; helps parents locate missing children; distributes photos and descriptions; and provides assistance to law enforcement agencies.

Child Find of America, Inc.   1-800-426-5678
Provides assistance and advice in locating missing children; national photo distribution and registration; information on prevention. Also assists parents return from hiding with abducted children.

Drugs and Alcohol

Alcohol Hotline
Alcoholics Anonymous/
Alanon/Alateen   1-800-ALCOHOL
Provides referrals to local support groups for alcoholics, families of alcoholics and teens who have parents or siblings with a drinking problem.

Cocaine Hotline   1-800-COCAINE
Provides information and referrals on drug abuse, not only cocaine.

Helpline
National Institute on Drug Abuse   1-800-662-HELP
Provides referrals for crisis intervention and treatment for substance abusers.

Pride Drug Information Line   1-800-241-9746
Provides drug information on substance abuse and referrals to local programs.

Health

AIDS Hotline
(U.S. Public Health Service)   1-800-342-AIDS
Provides information on AIDS and referrals for testing and counseling.

STD Hotline   1-800-227-8922
Provides information on sexually transmitted diseases like herpes, syphilis, gonorrhea, and referrals for testing and treatment.

National Health Information
Clearinghouse   1-800-336-4797
Provides information on a broad range of health issues.

Birthright   1-800-848-5683
  in New Jersey   1-609-848-1819
Provides referrals to local Birthright organizations which will assist pregnant women of all ages with support and counseling throughout their pregnancy.

Adolescent Suicide Hotline   1-800-621-4000
Provides Crisis intervention and referrals for young people considering suicide.

Coalitions/Networks

The list that follows includes state and regional coalitions of runaway and homeless youth serving agencies. Though these networks do not provide shelter or other services directly to young people, they can provide information about what is available in the state or the region and about the needs of homeless and runaway youth of that region.

Remember, Nineline, 1-800-999-9999, is always available to connect a young person directly to a program that can provide shelter or other direct services.

National

National Network of Runaway Youth Services
905 6th Street, S.W.
Suite 411

Washington, D.C.
(202) 488-0739

State and Regional

California Child, Youth and Family Coalition
2115 J Street, 18
Sacramento, CA 95816
(916) 443-2711
(800) 843-5200 (California Hotline)

Western States Youth Services
221 Petaluma Boulevard South
Petaluma, CA 94952
(707) 763-2213
(California, Arizona,
Nevada, Hawaii,
Pacific Territories)

Colorado Network of Runaway Youth Services
1240 W. Bayaud Avenue
Denver, CO 80228
(303) 698-2300
(800) 572-Home (Colorado Hotline)

Connecticut Youth Services Association
c/o Bristol Youth Services
111 N. Main Street
Bristol, CT 06010
(203) 584-7995

Florida Network of Youth and Family Services
804 E. Park Avenue
Tallahassee, FL 32301
(904) 222-4868

Hawaii Youth Services Network
Hale Kipa
2146 Damon Street
Honolulu, HI 96622
(808) 942-4989

Southeastern Network of Runaway Youth and Family Services
337 S. Miledge Avenue, Suite 209
Athens, GA 30605
(404) 354-4568
(Alabama, Florida, Georgia, Kentucky, Mississippi, North Carolina, South Carolina, Tennessee)

Mid-Atlantic Association of Youth Services
c/o Southern Area Youth Services
P.O. Box 44408
Friendly, MD 20744
(301) 292-3825

(800) 637-Kids (Maryland Hotline)
(District of Columbia, Virginia, Pennsylvania, Maryland, Delaware, West Virginia)

Illinois Collaboration on Youth
506 S. Wabash, Suite 520
Chicago, IL 60605
(312) 427-2710
(800) 972-6004 (Illinois Hotline)

Indiana Youth Services Association
c/o Crisis Center
101 N. Montgomery
Gary, IN 46403
(219) 938-7070

*Massachusetts Committee for Children/Coalition for
Adolescent Emergency Services and New
England Consortium for Families and Youth*
14 Beacon Street, Suite 706
Boston, MA 02108
(617) 742-8555
*(Maine, New Hampshire, Vermont, Massachusetts,
Rhode Island, Connecticut)*
(800) 792-5200 (Massachusetts Hotline)

Michigan Network of Runaway and Youth Services
115 W. Allegan, Suite 740
Lansing, MI 48933
(517) 484-5262
(800) 292-4517 (Michigan Hotline)

*M.I.N.K.
A Network of Runaway & Homeless Youth*
P.O. Box 12181
Parkville, MO 64152
(816) 741-8700
(Missouri, Iowa, Nebraska, Kansas)

Garden State Coalition of Youth and Family Concerns
P.O. Box 1401
Voorhees, NJ 08043
(609) 783-8355
(New Jersey, Puerto Rico, Virgin Islands)

New Mexico Youthworkers
c/o New Day
1817 Sigma Chi, NE

Albuquerque, NM 87106
(505) 247-9559

Empire State Coalition of Youth and Family Services
121 Avenue of the Americas
New York, NY 10013
(212) 941-9090

Mountain Plains Youth Services Network
311 N. Washington
Bismarck, ND 58501
(701) 255-7229
*(Montana, Wyoming, Colorado, Utah, North Dakota,
South Dakota)*

Ohio Youth Services Network
50 W. Broad Street, Suite 320
Columbus, OH 43215
(614) 461-1354

Oklahoma Association of Youth Services
125 N. Greenwood
Tulsa, OK 74120
(918) 585-2986
(800) 522-TEEN (Oklahoma Hotline)

Northwest Network of Runaway and Youth Services
94 Third Avenue
Ashland OR 97520
(503) 482-8890
(Washington, Oregon, Alaska, Idaho)

Youth Services Alliance of Pennsylvania
205 E. Beaver Avenue
State College, PA 16801
(814) 237-5731

Texas Network of Youth Services Southwest
Network of Youth Services
404 W. 40th St.
Austin, TX 78751
(512) 459-1455
(800) 392-3352 (Texas Hotline)
(Texas, New Mexico, Oklahoma, Arkansas, Louisiana)

Vermont Coalition and Youth Services Bureau
c/o Washington County Youth Service Bureau
38 Elm Street
Montpelier, VT 05602
(802) 229-9151

Alliance for Children, Youth and Families
172 29th Avenue
Seattle, WA 98122
(206) 324-0340

Wisconsin Association for Runaway Services
2318 E. Dayton Avenue
Madison, WI 53704
(608) 241-2649

Glossary

addiction Physical dependence upon something, such as alcohol or another drug.

AIDS (acquired immune deficiency syndrome) Virus that depresses the body's ability to fight infection and leads to many ailments that result in death.

anxiety Feeling of fear or uneasiness.

counseling Advice from a trained professional about personal problems and concerns.

depression Emotional state in which a person feels sad or dejected for an extended period of time and ceases to function normally.

downer Narcotic substance that severely depresses the central nervous system.

emotional abuse Deliberate manipulation of a person's feelings and emotions so that he feels negative about himself.

foster home Temporary home for children who have been legally separated from their parents.

group therapy Psychological treatment in which persons discuss their emotional problems with a small group of people and a therapist or counselor.

hustling Selling one's body to another person for sexual favors and acts.

john Person who pays another to engage in sexual acts for money.

nervous breakdown State of extreme emotional stress in which a person is unable to function normally.

peer Person who is of similar age and background.

physical abuse Mistreatment of a person's body by another, often leading to bruises and other injuries.

pimp Person who oversees and controls the activities of a prostitute.

prostitute Person who sells his or her body to another person for the purpose of performing sexual acts.

psychology Science that studies the human mind, emotions, and feelings.

residential care Place where a person lives in a group setting and receives help for his or her problems.

sexual abuse Mistreatment of a person by another through the forced performance of sexual acts.

sexual intercourse Intimate sexual act between two people involving the stimulation of the sexual organs or other body parts and the exchange of body fluids; can result in pregnancy.

shelter Place where a person can live temporarily and be protected from harsh or life-threatening circumstances.

sibling Brother or sister.

suicide Act of taking one's own life.

symptom Sign or indication of a disturbance or change within a person.

trick Paid sexual act performed by a prostitute.

uppers Narcotic substance that stimulates the central nervous system.

vaccine Medicine used to kill a virus.

venereal disease Contagious disease such as syphilis or gonorrhea, usually acquired through sexual intercourse with an infected person.

vial Small glass container for drugs such as crack.

virus Microscopic agent that enters the human bloodstream and causes illness or disease.

welt Raised lump of tissue caused by a heavy blow.

Index

A

addiction, 20, 21, 46–58
　crack, 59–67
advertising, influence of, 49
AIDS (acquired immune
　　deficiency syndrome), 22,
　23, 55, 57, 63, 65, 77, 81–
　85, 93
Alanon, 92
Alateen, 29, 53, 92
alcohol
　abuse of, 21, 31, 48–52
　used with drugs, 66
anxiety, coping with, 95–96

B

baby, arrival of, 20, 41
Birthright, 86–87
blackout, memory, 51

C

child abuse, 4, 17, 31–32, 34–
　45
　abuser as victim of, 31, 41
choices
　dead-end, 21
　good, 5–6
cocaine, 13, 55, 59
　freebase, 61
communication
　open, 3, 4, 24, 89
　problems, 72

counselor
　Covenant House, 2, 14, 44
　family service, 30, 53
　hospital, 74
courage, 9, 15, 26, 44, 45
Covenant House, 1, 4, 16, 20,
　43, 57, 63, 65, 83, 98
crack, 54, 55, 59–67
curfew, 15

D

death
　from AIDS, 84
　alcohol-related, 50–51
　from drug overdose, 22, 55,
　57
　drug-related, 65

decisions, making, 88–89, 97–
　98
dependence
　on alcohol, 50
　on drugs, 54–55
　on parents, 42
depression, 40, 51, 56, 75
discipline, vs. abuse, 4, 38, 40–
　41
disease, sexually transmitted
　　(STD), 23
divorce, 20, 32, 91
drinking, 17, 26–27
　adolescent, 46–47

and driving, 50
drugs, 10, 13
   abuse of, 21, 27, 31, 48
   addiction to, 20, 54–58
   dealing, 37, 60, 62

E
emotional abuse, 21, 27, 30, 31,
   38, 40
escape
   drinking as, 50
   from problems, 21
experimentation, with drugs, 54

F
father
   abusive, 17
   fighting with, 26–27
fighting
   parental, 48, 91
   parent-child, 32, 39
foster home, 13, 19
friends
   changing, 58
   inability to make, 40
   making, 79–80
   problems with, 93–94
frustration, 26–27, 97

G
gonorrhea, 23, 81, 93

H
hallucinogens, 57
help
   asking for, 2, 15, 23, 25, 29, 32
   need for, 45, 97
   professional, 56, 75
   suicide as cry for, 70–71, 75

hepatitis, 51, 55, 57
heroin, 9, 13, 57, 61
hotline, tollfree, 1, 2, 45, 98
hustling, 60, 73

I
immediacy, 5
infection, in sexual abuse, 39–40

J
john, 8, 9

L
Love
   for abuser, 31
   inappropriate expression of,
     41
   parental, 42
   search for, 18
   unconditional, 5
LSD, 54, 59

M
marijuana, 55–56, 59
myths, about suicide, 69–71

N
Nineline, 1, 2, 20, 26, 30, 53,
   57, 60, 75, 97–98

O
overdose, drug, 22
overprotectiveness, 90

P
panic reaction, 56
parents
   with alcohol/drug problem, 92
   calling Nineline, 3, 4

nagging, 90
PCP, 57
peer pressure, 21–22, 77–87
Phoenix House, 55
physical abuse, 21, 31, 38–39, 92
pimp, 10, 12–13
pneumonia, 51, 84
pregnancy, 22, 40, 81, 85–87, 93
pressure
    to drink, 49, 93
    family, 20, 32
    of responsibility, 27–28
principles, Covenant House, 4–6
problems
    family, 18, 20, 25, 29
    parental, 31
    school, 94–95
    working out, 7
prostitution, 8, 12–13, 22–23, 37, 60, 62, 63, 64–65
"pushout," 19
put-downs, 41, 78

R
rape, 10
relationships, family, 20, 29
remarriage, parent's, 10, 32, 91–92
respect, absolute, 5
responsibility, assuming, 28, 30, 32, 72, 86–87
runaways, types of, 18–20

S
sanctuary, 5
self-blame, 31, 32, 42
sex
    abstaining from, 85
    decisions about, 22, 78, 81–82, 84, 94
    pressure about, 93–94
sexual abuse, 21, 38–40, 69, 74, 92
sexual intercourse, 39, 85
shelter
    Covenant House, 61, 63
    temporary, 13, 18
speed, 13, 59
stealing, 36–37, 62
stepparent, 10, 20, 91–92
stress
    family, 20, 41
    financial, 32, 41
    normal, in family, 3, 30
structure, of solution, 5
suicide, 21, 68–76
syphilis, 23, 81, 93

T
THC, 56
"throwaway," 19
tolerance, of alcohol, 51, 52
treatment program
    alcohol, 46, 53
    drug, 62–63, 66
trick, 8, 64
    "sick," 22
trust, lack of, 9, 36

V
values
    communication of, 5
    twisted, 19, 34, 36
van, outreach, 63, 64
violence, street, 64–65

W

warning signs

   of alcohol problem, 51–52

   of family problem, 21–33

   of running away, 20–22

of suicide, 71–73

withdrawal

   alcohol, 52

   as escape, 35, 73